Crisis and Change

Crisis and Change

My Years as President of the
Unitarian Universalist Association, 1969–1977

Robert Nelson West

SKINNER HOUSE BOOKS

BOSTON

Printed in the United States

ISBN 1-55896-521-1
978-1-55896-521-8

5 4 3 2
09 08

Library of Congress Cataloging-in-Publication Data

West, Robert Nelson.
  Crisis and change : my years as president of the Unitarian
Universalist Association, 1969-1977 / Robert Nelson West.
     p. cm.
  Includes index.
  ISBN-13: 978-1-55896-521-8 (pbk. : alk. paper)
  ISBN-10: 1-55896-521-1 (pbk. : alk. paper) 1. West, Robert Nelson.
2. Unitarian Universalist Association--Presidents—Biography. 3.
Unitarian Universalist Association—History. I. Title.

BX9869.W48A3 2007
289.1092—dc22
[B]

2006035056

To those who brought
and kept the free faith.

Contents

Foreword

BOB WEST is given to understatement.

"Crisis" hardly describes what he was up against after taking office as the second president of the Unitarian Universalist Association. He discovered that his predecessor, having already spent all non-restricted funds and run up a deficit, had at the last minute taken out a bank loan subject to immediate repayment without letting his successor know. Then, a few years later, in response to the publication by Beacon Press of the *Pentagon Papers*, a grand jury was about to have Bob indicted. Someone less restrained might describe looming bankruptcy or the threat of jail as a shade more serious than a crisis.

Nor does "change" begin to suggest the scope of the UUA reorganization that Bob was forced to undertake. Since he leans over backwards to be fair, he plays down the often destructive opposition and personal vilification he encountered. Finally, Bob's ingrained modesty does not permit him to claim due credit for the degree to which it was his personal intervention that brought about the course reversal of which so many had despaired, beginning with his willingness to run for an office that promised nothing but problems and pain.

Unencumbered by such compunctions, I can't help but experience the emotions of those turbulent times over again as I read

Bob's recollections. First as president of the Metropolitan New York District and then as the district's representative on the UUA board, I was filled with admiration for Bob's imaginative and courageous leadership, and distress at the way the denomination was indulging in often hurtful infighting. While I did not always agree with Bob on specifics, I watched with growing respect his steadfastness, his courtesy, and the outward calm with which he encountered his (and our) tribulations.

The UUA's survival was by no means a foregone conclusion. To save us from shipwreck, Bob had to start his presidency by terminating five of eight department heads and shutting down all district offices. Those cuts, however essential, did not make friends, and they explain in part the virulent abuse directed at both at the UUA and at Bob personally. Meanwhile, the gut-wrenching disagreements about how best to respond to the cry for racial justice further eroded our denomination's cohesion and effectiveness.

If all this seems like hyperbole, consider this: The same General Assembly that elected Bob West was marked by walkouts, microphone seizures, and vicious invective, with ministerial colleagues spitting in each others' faces.

Readers who did not live through the 1970s may wonder how we could have deviated so far from our basic principles of tolerance and mutual respect, or how it was possible for the Nixon administration to use every legal and extra-legal attempt to intimidate and silence us. Keep this context in mind as you read Bob's story in order to fully appreciate his achievement; under his leadership we not only persevered and began to heal our wounds but laid the groundwork for going on to greater strength and a deeper appreciation of our faith.

But there is more, for in addition to tackling inherited problems, Bob also launched several initiatives that transformed the denomination. For instance, Bob overcame the understandable skepticism of the Shelter Rock congregation about the UUA's trustworthiness, thus tapping into a flood of generosity that has made a huge difference in the vibrancy and effectiveness of our denomination. This may be the most important achievement of Bob's administration in terms of lasting impact, followed closely by the launch of *UU World*, our first denominational periodical sent at no charge to every active member family of every UU congregation. For the first time, all Unitarian Universalists were able to find out what was happening in the denomination and what their elected leaders were doing and saying and to voice their own opinions, creating an unprecedented sense of belonging to a larger religious family, of seeing beyond our parochial walls.

If you need a third example, pick any one of these: professionalizing the Association's personnel policies, putting an end to cronyism on the Association's board, or setting new standards and increasing professional recognition for our religious educators.

The years of Bob's presidency were tumultuous, certainly, but he managed to bring joy and celebration to the work as well. Bob and Nancy West gave great parties. At least once during each board meeting they invited the trustees to their apartment on Beacon Hill to share in their gracious hospitality. The highlight came when Bob passed out Methodist hymnals and sat with Nancy at the piano. Nancy is a professional musician but Bob matched her in enthusiasm; together they led a crowd of dedicated UUs as they belted out old revival favorites. That's when all agenda problems, all ideological confrontations and machinations were forgotten. At these times we realized the warmth and empathy that underlay Bob's highly self-contained and self-disciplined demeanor.

The next morning it was back to problems, but whether the problem was budget cutting or the FBI rifling through the UUA's bank records, Bob's decisive and principled leadership enabled him to begin to heal the wounds of a badly divided denomination and organize a national coalition in defense of freedom of speech and of religion.

Yes, those were tough times and in many ways not our proudest hours. As you read Bob's dispassionate descriptions, keep in mind that if his narrative has any flaw it's that he makes it all sound too easy. That's Bob. Even in the darkest moment, when the survival of the UUA was at risk, he never raised his voice or asked for sympathy, never sought to put the blame on others or pay back his tormentors.

But Bob's successes came at great cost to himself. When his second term was over, he withdrew from all denominational activities and took a year off in England, then switched careers. Except for conducting a memorial service for Paul Carnes in 1979, he did not even attend another General Assembly until 2003, so we should be especially grateful that we now have this first-hand account of the historic events that shaped our merged denomination.

The story told in these pages is inspiring, but it also has a grim timeliness. In the 1970s, Bob sounded a warning about a government that played on citizens' fears and used "'national security' and 'criminal activity' as excuses to suspend the Constitution and violate historic guarantees of freedom." In 1974 he wrote of Gerald Ford that he would "better serve our nation if he resists the temptation to equate his decisions with those of the deity."

Equally prescient is Bob's description of his initiative to explore and define Unitarian Universalist identity, an articulation he felt was "necessary if we are to be more effective" and thereby strengthen our motivation and cohesiveness.

This book can once again help us come closer to that goal, so thank you, Bob, for all you did back then, and thank you for sharing your story.

Warren Ross

Preface

The time of my tenure as president of the Unitarian Universalist Association of Congregations was like no other in our Unitarian and Universalist history. The years from 1969 to 1977 were a contentious time in American life as well, the momentous reverberations of which continue to echo through critical national and international events today.

The UUA is a voluntary association that was formed by the 1961 consolidation of the American Unitarian Association and the Universalist Church of America. These two denominations dated back to the early nineteenth and late eighteenth centuries, respectively. I was elected by delegates from member congregations who meet annually in a General Assembly to conduct the Association's business. I served for two four-year terms, succeeding the denomination's first president, Dana McLean Greeley, who was in office from 1961 to 1969.

Although it has elements of both, this account is intended neither as an institutional history nor as a personal memoir. Its genesis was an invitation from the late Peter Raible, the then president of the Unitarian Universalist Retired Ministers and Partners Association, to give an address during the 2003 General Assembly reflecting on the "often turbulent and stressful years" of my two terms. To ensure the accuracy of events and dates, I reviewed all the back issues of *UUA Now* magazine and the *UU World* newspaper from 1968 to 1977, as well as many archived documents from that era.

A compelling motivation for me to tell this story was the present-day lack of knowledge in our denomination about that period. If I were to choose only one word to characterize everything that occurred during my presidency, it would be *change*, institutional change from the way things had been done for the first eight years of the UUA's existence. I believe the years covered by this book put our denomination on track for what it would be over the next several decades. I hope the unique perspective of the president during those years can help today's members of our religious movement gain a better understanding of why some things are as they are as we progress into the future.

Robert Nelson West
April 2007

The Campaign

JUNE 1968 FOUND ME nearing the end of five years as minister of the First Unitarian Church in Rochester, New York, and our denomination nearing the time to choose its second president, who would succeed Dana Greeley. Simultaneously, three forces were converging in the Unitarian Universalist Association: a crisis caused by the financial practices of the outgoing administration, the vote at our May 1968 General Assembly to give $250 thousand annually to the Black Affairs Council (BAC) for four years, and the surge of anti-institutionalism and confrontational politics in American society and our denomination. Some candidates had already begun their election campaigns, and I was approached that spring by a number of people who urged me to run as well. At the time, I wasn't interested.

The 1968–1969 campaign was marked by intense and often bitter controversy about the best way to approach racial divisiveness within Unitarian Universalism. Was it better to support an exclusively black group working for self-determination, or a group of black and white UUs working together, or both? The principal organizations advocating the separatist approach were BAC and the Black Unitarian Universalist Caucus (BUUC). The primary organization urging the integrationist approach was Black and White Action (BAWA).

There was also strong dissatisfaction on the part of many concerning the financial practices of the UUA administration and board. Besides voting on the BAC contribution—a total amount equivalent to $6 million today—the assembly had voted to spend additional money that wasn't in the UUA budget, for example, to establish an independent journal of liberal religion and to significantly increase theological school allocations. Association bylaws vested the UUA board with final authority to take any of these actions.

The BAC funding controversy somewhat overshadowed the individual election campaigns already in progress. For several years, Paul Carnes, minister of the Buffalo church in New York, had been considered the leading probable candidate for the 1969 election, but for health reasons he declined to run. The two leading contenders in the summer of 1968 were Harry Scholefield, minister of the San Francisco church, and Robert Hohler, executive director of the Unitarian Universalist Laymen's League.

Paul Carnes was especially insistent that I run and volunteered to be my campaign manager. I promised to think about it during the summer and let him know my decision. At that time, I was spending most of each summer with my family at a lakeside cabin, a mile down a dirt road from the paved highway. The nearest village was eight miles away, and we had no telephone.

For the greater part of the summer, I carefully considered running for the office of UUA president. In August, I decided not to run and sent a telegram to Paul. Relieved, I went on to enjoy the rest of my vacation. After I returned home in early September, I learned that Paul hadn't received the telegram because he was traveling in Europe. Over the next few days, we talked intensely about our denomination in general and the campaigns already under way. The result was that I announced my candidacy on September 12.

I was thirty-nine, and the persuading factor in deciding to run was my concern that a young candidate would be elected. The crisis in our denomination was affecting programs, finances, attitudes, and identity. I believed that our priorities needed to be more comprehensive and balanced than those advocated by the younger candidates. Harry Scholefield, from an earlier generation than mine and with profoundly impressive personal qualities, would have been my preference. I planned to drop out if he led the race at a late stage in the campaign. Events quickly made that plan moot: A few days after I announced my candidacy, Harry Scholefield and Robert Hohler declared they were no longer in the race.

Being the sole candidate felt strange, but in the course of the next few weeks, six others joined me. They were Carleton Fisher, minister of the church in Freeport, New York, and a former president of the Universalist Church of America; John Fisher, minister of churches in Eastham and Brewster, Massachusetts; Aron Gilmartin, minister of the Walnut Creek, California, church; Harold Hadley, minister of the church in Plandome, New York; Philip Larson, minister of the Newport, Rhode Island, church; and Deane Starr, UUA vice president for field services and former minister of churches in Acton and Harvard, Massachusetts.

Direct in conversation and comfortable sharing criticism, Paul Carnes was an outstanding campaign manager and the major factor in creating a highly effective campaign organization. Christopher Raible, minister of the Milwaukee church and formerly Harry Scholefield's campaign manager, agreed to be campaign coordinator. He had keen organizing skills and did a superb job. Given their busy lives as parish ministers, Paul and Chris worked exceptionally hard for my candidacy, prodding me whenever they believed it was necessary. Our campaign organization was simple, yet comprehensive: a layperson and minister as co-chairs in every UUA district and Canada, assisted by several regional coordinators, all responsible for enlisting other supporters in their respective areas. The result was that a substantial number of people spent a significant amount of time and effort on the campaign—and I'm grateful to them still.

Prior to that September, the UUA had paid the BAC $250 thousand of the $1 million voted by the 1968 General Assembly. At least three of the seven presidential candidates favored a guarantee that another $250 thousand would be taken off the top of the UUA annual budget in each of the next three years and paid to the BAC, regardless of what else might occur.

My approach was different. In my campaign brochure, I pointed out that our movement was in a severe crisis involving programs, finances, attitudes, and identity and that we must gain a new sense of direction. I emphasized that the primary purpose of the UUA was to serve local congregations. I also stated, "Some blacks and whites in our denomination believe they can deal most effectively with our racial ills through black self-determination. Others believe that, for their part, the most effective method is to work together, black and white. I would support this pluralism among us." I was committed to securing the remaining $750 thousand over the next three years, but rather than raising the amount through our UUA annual fund, I advocated special voluntary campaigns among congregations and individuals.

Seeing a $650-thousand deficit in a budget of some $2.7 million —with almost all of our unrestricted capital gone—as an immediate crisis that must be faced, I emphasized these basic questions: What are the essential functions of our continental organization? What does the UUA *have* to do? I urged that we identify three or four priorities and implement them well—then use any remaining money for additional things we might *like* to do.

I named four essential UUA functions: leadership standards, religious education, social responsibility, and improved communication. Leadership standards included recruiting and training ministers and religious education directors, and maintaining the quality of our professional leadership. It also involved developing lay leadership, an increasingly vital factor in the life of our congregations. Concerning religious education, I suggested that the new direction in our curriculum materials seemed sound and should be continued, as should our new program for accreditation of religious education directors, but that both were underfinanced and should be given greater support.

Social responsibility entails putting our religion into practice, and I said we should recognize that most effective social action occurs in local communities. While we do need some continental representation for social responsibility, I saw the larger role of the UUA as facilitator, stimulator, and communicator for local efforts. What we needed were improved means to share information among local groups and to provide the support of resource people.

Concerning improved communication, I emphasized our need to share significant events of local congregations, whether social action endeavors or creative worship or curriculum development. In the brochure, I wrote, "We have no common experience as a denomination. There is an information blockage. A balanced, good newspaper in all of our homes would be a great aid—particularly if much space were devoted to a vigorous exchange of opinion and thought."

The brochure's closing statement emphasized that nourishing and supplementing personal religion must be at the center not only of congregations but also of our denomination. During the entire campaign, I stressed that the UUA administration and board must begin to set annual budgets that reasonably reflect the anticipated annual income and that the Association must operate every year on a balanced budget based on realistic projections of expected income.

This excerpt from an address in February 1969 conveyed a core message of my candidacy:

> Our UUA must be a strong, viable continental religious movement worthy of the name. We are needed—and we will be needed more in the next ten years. I hold out to you no starry-eyed, impossible, and unattainable vision. I do say that we will make our contribution if we stand fast on the unique principles and ideals of our movement: individual freedom, individual conscience, the dignity of the individual, and a practical concern for the actual conditions of human beings.

The 1969 General Assembly met in Boston in the third week of July. During a morning business session, each of the seven presidential candidates had ten minutes to address the delegates before polls opened for voting. I recently discovered the handwritten text of my talk, and I believe a portion of it reflects the collegial nature of the candidates' personal relationships:

> As I think back over those months of the campaign, memories and impressions cross my mind. I recall such events as the night in a motel when Deane won: He and I flipped and I was the one who had to sleep with Carleton Fisher. I found out that Carleton snores. I recall the blizzards in New England. And the people who told me there was no need to take my rubbers to Seattle—and the six inches of snow that greeted me. I remember an enjoyable ride in a jet from New Orleans to San Francisco with Gil, a quiet break in the campaign. And the weeks it took me to talk Harold Hadley into flying with me over the Adirondacks in a small plane. That's when I discovered that Deane gets airsick in light aircraft. And I remember his saying that had he known the flight was going to be so bumpy, he would have eaten cherry pie instead of a hot dog before we took off.
>
> I remember publicly disagreeing at times with Phil and Jack, but privately our being able to maintain an open and amiable relationship. One of the aspects of the campaign about which I feel best is the personal relationships that have been maintained among all seven candidates in spite of the intense pressures and at times sharp disagreement on some issues. I believe that what has enabled us to maintain such a relationship is our common concern for this free religious movement of ours, our deep conviction of the need by persons for a liberal religious movement, and of our need, all of us, for one another.

When the ballots were tallied and certified, I had received more than half the votes. It was fortunate that the election results were so decisive. Otherwise, I believe the divisions within our denomination might have become deeper.

After the General Assembly, Nancy and I accepted the invitation of friends from our former congregation to accompany them sailing for two weeks. We recuperated from ten months of campaigning combined with ministerial responsibilities in Rochester, and then we moved our family of six to Boston.

Financial Crisis and Organizational Changes

WHEN I WALKED into my new office at 25 Beacon Street in the summer of 1969, my most immediate problem was the Association's financial predicament. The same General Assembly that elected me also voted that the UUA spend more money for theological schools, Chicanos, religious education programs, our United Nations office, and the Canadian Unitarian Council. Yet the delegates overwhelmingly passed a resolution urging the board of trustees "most strongly" to move as rapidly as possible to a balanced budget for the Association based on realistic projections of expected income.

We were well into a fiscal year that began several weeks before I was elected. Our annual operating budget was $2.6 million with income of only $1.6 million, and the outgoing administration had spent all unrestricted capital.

I immediately implemented a major reorganization and a $1-million budget cut that reduced the UUA staff by half and the budget by 40 percent. I met with the trustees in September to acquaint them with our dilemma, and I agreed to prepare specific recommendations for coping with the situation. I also met with the presidents of all the districts. Intertwined with the financial crisis, yet separate, was the controversy over whether to fund the Black Affairs Council (BAC) for the entire annual amount voted at the 1968 General Assembly.

In developing my budget and reorganization recommendations, I focused on preserving and enhancing programs and services that were most likely to help local congregations with basic
needs, which included recruiting and training ministers and religious education directors, maintaining the quality of professional
leadership, publishing religious education curriculum materials,
helping congregations be more effective in social action, developing lay leadership, and sharing information and improving communication between congregations and the UUA. I had stated in
my campaign brochure that the UUA "is a family of congregations
and is the continental expression of our free religious movement.
Its primary purpose is to serve local congregations . . . to develop
programs and services our members need and want." That was
one of the three guiding principles uppermost in my mind
throughout those challenging years. The other two were the ideals
of our Unitarian Universalist movement and the long-term health
of our denomination.

The trustees approved my proposed plan at a special mid-
November meeting. The only significant disagreement during
their deliberations was the total amount to be paid BAC in the
1969–1970 fiscal year. The board approved cutting $1 million in
programs and staff—a 40-percent reduction in the budget, equivalent today to slashing nearly $6 million from an operating budget
of about $15 million. We reduced the number of UUA staff mem-
bers from 108 to 55, leaving roughly one-fourth the number of
today's UUA staff members to serve approximately the same number of congregations. Five of the eight department heads at UUA
headquarters were terminated and departmental functions combined. The reorganization entailed terminating all employees—
executive directors and support staff—in the twenty-one districts
of the UUA. We grouped the districts into seven interdistrict
councils, each with its own full-time interdistrict representative
who was a UUA staff member—not an executive or administrator
but a resource person who lived in the region and concentrated
primarily on helping congregations improve local programs, with

special emphasis on extension and lay leadership development. To provide local assistance to congregations that needed new ministers, the board approved appointing a ministerial settlement representative to every district, a qualified volunteer whose expenses would be reimbursed by the Association. The trustees eliminated eighteen UUA committees.

The proposals approved at the special November meeting included other modifications and innovations. The board voted to create the *UU World* newspaper as our UUA journal and suspend publication of *UUA Now* magazine. We discontinued the monthly information packet and nearly all other general mailings from UUA headquarters. The Church of the Larger Fellowship, with approximately four thousand members, was eliminated as a function of headquarters and established as a separate congregation, with the UUA agreeing to contribute funds only as required to assure continuing viability. We significantly curtailed the Association's public relations and information programs and abolished the Office of Overseas and Interfaith Relations (see the chapter "International Activities").

Financial support of Liberal Religious Youth, the denomination's high-school-age organization, was reduced by one-third, as was funding for the college-age group, Student Religious Liberals. We eliminated financial assistance to the Unitarian Universalist Women's Federation and Unitarian Universalist Laymen's League, but continued to provide free space, heat, and electricity for all four organizations. The allocation for our United Nations Office in New York was reduced. We were able to retain the Washington Office for Social Concern by sharing funding and space with the American Ethical Union and American Humanist Association.

Two months after the November board meeting, believing we had at last managed to cope with our appalling financial situation, I was dismayed to discover that our bank held an open demand note for $450 thousand. The last $50 thousand of the note had been borrowed two weeks before the General Assembly at which I was elected and after our new fiscal year had begun, yet several top officials of the prior administration told me they had no knowledge of the note. In January 1970, the new treasurer and I met with the bank vice president who was responsible for monitoring the loan and promised him we would apply the full amount of every unrestricted bequest the Association received until the note was retired.

Besides developing the recommendations that the trustees approved in November, I took other steps toward enhancing the Association's financial health. I instituted, and stringently applied, two policies concerning budgets and loans: No UUA annual budget was ever to be higher than the amount of income that was realistically expected, and no such borrowing as the $450-thousand "mystery" note was to occur again.

At that time, many people had lost confidence in the UUA administration and were reluctant to give money—the annual program fund goal had not been achieved for the last three years. Contributions were also adversely affected by the rancorous controversies swirling in the denomination. I traveled to as many areas as possible of the United States and Canada, explaining the UUA situation, listening to members of local congregations, and answering questions. My purpose wasn't only to convey information about what we were doing and to hear the views of our members firsthand but also to build confidence in our Association.

On several occasions early in my first term a number of people pressed us to sell all the real estate associated with UUA headquarters in Boston as a way out of our financial difficulties, and the board ultimately appointed a special committee to investigate the matter. In October 1971, this committee reported that if our headquarters properties were sold, the cost of rent would wipe out the entire profit within five years. The board accepted the committee's report, took no action, and to my knowledge such proposals were not mentioned again in my tenure.

I was concerned about our organizational health as well. Shortly after I came to office, the president of the UUA employees organization visited me with a request from headquarters staff members: that I examine and improve upon the departing administration's practices in determining annual salaries. He reported that most employees believed annual compensation depended to a large extent on one's personal relationship with administration officials, and that a system with fair and equitable standards and guidelines was preferable.

I readily agreed to their request and engaged the services of a respected compensation consultant who happened to be a Unitarian Universalist. After conducting extensive interviews, reviewing the duties of each position, and examining payroll records, the consultant found that the compensation of a significant number of our staff members was either higher or lower than he deemed appropriate by generally accepted standards. He proposed a salary administration system that considered the type of duties involved, the individual's experience and quality of performance, and the current compensation for performing similar duties in comparable positions around the Boston area. I immediately instituted this plan and designated a staff person to be personnel coordinator.

During those early months of my first term, I found that membership figures published in UUA directories by the Greeley administration for the past several years were significantly inflated. I believed strongly that our published information should reflect actual circumstances as accurately as possible. With the assistance of our headquarters and field staff and the cooperation of most congregations, I undertook a comprehensive effort to have our published membership numbers reflect reality. One congregation had been listed as having 45 hundred members, but reliable sources reported its usual Sunday morning attendance to be less than a hundred. We removed 120 inactive congregations from the total membership figures and reduced the membership count of many active churches.

An often-overlooked occurrence of major significance was the dramatic change in the organizational relationship of districts to UUA headquarters. This change was brought about in 1969 by the actions taken because of our financial crisis and the amended bylaws that allowed individual districts to elect the overwhelming majority of UUA board members.

Before 1969, all districts in our denomination had executive offices staffed with paid employees. Some districts operated independently, often competing rather than cooperating with the continental Association of which they were part. A few possessed their own capital funds. However, the severe 1969 UUA budget cuts, staff reductions, and reorganization transformed the situation. Accompanying that development was the implementation of a major change, approved by earlier General Assemblies, whereby 77 percent of UUA board voting members were elected by individual districts—previously there were none.

Having individual districts elect most UUA trustees places on our congregations the responsibility of choosing sound and capable people, and I believe it has been beneficial.

I believe that at the time I entered office, the UUA board was more a creature of the president than it should have been. However, district elections of UUA trustees were beginning to be implemented and the situation improved. We created a larger meeting space for trustees at our headquarters building and opened all board meetings to observers.

The September 1969 board meeting was the first time that trustees who were elected by individual districts served as UUA board members. I'm sure many of them were shocked by the starkness and depth of the financial problems I conveyed at that meeting, as well as by my recommendations to cope with those difficulties. I was proud of the trustees' performance as they confronted the painful problems of that period. Their accomplishments on behalf of our denomination during that meeting and the two that followed were highly commendable.

Two additional initiatives I undertook were in relation to the Veatch program of the Unitarian Universalist congregation in Plandome, New York, and the Holdeen trusts. (See the chapter "The Veatch Program and Holdeen Trusts" for a detailed discussion of these initiatives.)

Recently I've been asked, "How did the UUA get into such an appalling financial situation? Why did the 1968 and 1969 General Assemblies vote to give away money the UUA did not have? Why did no one stand up at those General Assemblies and describe the true financial circumstances?" It's my recollection that some did stand up and say that the UUA didn't have the money, but they were hooted down, ignored, or not believed.

For eight years—since its inception—the UUA had followed a policy of deficit spending that the leadership justified as an investment in the future: The idea was that more money spent would produce more members, and more members would produce more money. That scenario never materialized. There was no substantial increase in our total membership. Meanwhile the UUA spent more than $5 million from its development fund and unrestricted capital to cover budget shortfalls every year, but those resources ran out as the Greeley administration was leaving office.

At the 1968 General Assembly in Cleveland, the UUA administration and board didn't reveal the precariousness of the financial situation. In the minds of UUA leaders, there was always hope that something would occur to rescue the denomination from financial misery.

The delegates in Cleveland were caught up in a right-sounding cause. They were confused by the total amount of capital (restricted and unrestricted) shown in the financial reports. Most of the delegates had little patience for financial details—after all, the UUA had continued functioning each year despite the naysaying of financial critics. Emotion and fervor overcame reality. There was an overpowering mood of "you are either for us or against us." Those who attempted to mention financial reasons for not supporting an action were considered to be against the high ideals of an admirable cause. The same kind of dynamic operated in the 1969 General Assembly at Boston, except it was intensified by the presidential election and the one-day BAC walkout (see the chapter "Black UU Caucus and Black Affairs Council").

At the time of the 1968 General Assembly, the UUA administration and board were aware of our grave financial situation and
had the opportunity to deal with it before it became worse, but
they chose not to follow that course. The treasurer reported at the
board meeting of June 21–22, 1968, that if the annual program
fund (on which the UUA depended for more than half its operating income) fell short of its goal as he expected it would, the unrestricted funds of the Association might have to be completely
expended during the 1968–1969 fiscal year. He said that without
having a balance of unrestricted funds on hand, the UUA would
be forced to change its operations and programs beginning in the
1969–1970 fiscal year.

Nevertheless the administration recommended approval of a
budget based on an unrealistic increase in expected voluntary
contributions: 53 percent greater than the amount received the
preceding year. Speaking on behalf of the Greeley administration
in support of the proposed budget, the UUA treasurer said that it
was "impractical at this time to try to save money in the
1968–1969 fiscal year by further program cuts." In effect, that approach left the truly difficult financial decisions to the next administration, while exhausting the unrestricted capital. Still, the
trustees adopted the budget by a close vote.

Would the UUA have been better off if it had not promised in
Cleveland what it was unable to deliver? I believe the answer is
clearly yes. Our Association would have been immensely better off
if the financial truth had been told and believed in Cleveland in
1968: The UUA didn't have $1 million to fund BAC. Then the del-
egates and individual members of congregations would have had
to determine how they could realistically and effectively address
the racial problems about which people felt so strongly, rather
than returning home believing that the UUA could do it.

If the delegates at Cleveland wished to put $1 million into the
hands of a group to meet a critical need, they could have voted to
create a special vehicle to obtain the amount from congregations

and individual members, with the UUA contributing to the reasonable extent of its ability. Had they followed that course, our Association would have been spared much of the bitterness that ensued and from which it still suffers to some degree.

Moderator

Elected at large by the General Assembly for a four-year term, the moderator's duties are to preside at General Assemblies and meetings of the board and its executive committee, and to represent the Association on special occasions. Joseph Fisher, the moderator during my term in office, had impressive careers in education, economics, conservation, and government, including high positions at local, state, regional, and federal levels—and he is remembered and respected throughout our denomination for his steady, wise leadership.

As moderator from 1965 to 1977, Dr. Fisher presided at the unusually contentious 1968 and 1969 General Assemblies, as well as all the subsequent assemblies and most trustees' meetings mentioned in this book. In 1974, voters from the Tenth Congressional District of Virginia elected him to the U.S. House of Representatives, where he was an influential member of the powerful Ways and Means Committee throughout his three terms in Congress. We were blessed that Joseph Fisher was UUA moderator during an especially critical period in our history. We all are deeply indebted to him for the immense contribution of his talents and person to the cause of liberal religion.

Canada

The Canadian Unitarian Council (CUC) was organized in 1961 for the purpose of attending to matters unique to Canadian congregations, such as the application of religious and social actions to Canadian institutions, publications, and government.

Each Canadian congregation was in one of the six UUA districts situated along that nation's southern border, and U.S.

congregations constituted a heavy majority in all six. In the fall of 1969, I attended the CUC annual meeting and proposed that all Canada be a single district with its own Canadian office and staff funded by the UUA. The Canadians' response to my offer was intensely negative so I dropped the possibility. However, even after instituting the massive 1969 budget cuts, we managed to retain an annual level of UUA financial support for the CUC and its existing Ottawa office.

The 1970 General Assembly changed our Association's bylaws to require that one trustee elected at large always be from Canada. In 1972, UUA moderator Joseph Fisher and I met with CUC leaders and reached unanimous agreement concerning fundraising and sharing; we all recognized the importance of cooperation between the CUC and UUA for the benefit of our entire denomination.

Today there appears to be a general perception that my tenure was front-loaded with problems; unfortunately that wasn't the case, though I wish it had been. Some of the troubles we experienced were related to the financial and reorganizational difficulties that continued through my first six years. There were two economic recessions, one of them still cited as the worst since the Great Depression; inflation was a pervasive negative presence; and congregations did not contribute enough to the annual program fund to reach the modest goals. The fact that other denominations were undergoing the same experience wasn't much solace. In each of those first six years, we had to cut the UUA budget and implement reorganizations that affected programs, services, and staff members.

The worst year for cuts after 1969 was probably 1975. In developing the 1975 recommendations, I invited the entire UUA staff to make suggestions and also engaged an outside consultant. My resulting proposal, which the trustees approved by a 16–8 vote, reduced the number of executive staff positions at headquarters from six to three, eliminated some other positions, and combined our six departments into three.

During my presidency, I did not recommend undertaking any capital fundraising campaigns, nor to my knowledge did anyone else in our denomination. There were three primary reasons: Too many people had strongly negative feelings about the preceding administration's campaigns and the way the funds raised were spent; the general economy suffered two recessions; and there were too many divisions and negative attitudes among our membership resulting from events such as the Black Affairs Council controversies, the 1969 UUA presidential election, and the Vietnam War.

Throughout my tenure, the Association depended on the annual program fund for most of its current operating income. The annual goal had not been met during the previous administration's last three years and wasn't achieved during my first six years. Yet during each of my eight years in office, we held to the policy of operating on current income with balanced budgets. By 1973, we were completely out of debt, and when I left office the UUA was in sound financial condition.

Looking back on those initial months, I concur with Ed Darling's words in the final issue of *UUA Now* magazine. He said the crisis facing our movement was real, but it was "basically financial, and not a sickness of spirit, purpose, or commitment."

Black UU Caucus and
Black Affairs Council

THROUGHOUT MY EARLY YEARS in office, our precarious financial condition was closely entwined with the urgent issue of how best to use our resources in the cause of racial justice. At the crux of a continuing and pervasive controversy were the 1968 General Assembly vote to give $1 million to the Black Affairs Council (BAC) and, more specifically, whether the funds would come from UUA annual budgets or from voluntary contributions. Our membership—narrowly and intensely divided—faced the excruciating choice of whether to jeopardize the continuation of effective denominational functions in order to fund one particular approach to a worthy social objective. The majority sentiment of UUA board members expressed in April 1970 was that the Association's survival was the issue. Once more, our predicament demonstrated that the tension between our financial resources and the desire to fulfill the prophetic call of our religious heritage is never far from the surface.

The Black Unitarian Universalist Caucus (BUUC) was formed in 1967 and legally established in February 1968. BAC was incorporated in June 1968 by Hayward Henry, Dick Traylor, and Sam Beecher. The BAC bylaws specified two classes of membership. Class-A members (eleven people) were the BAC board members; they had voting rights and constituted the Black Affairs Council. Class-B members were the members of BUUC; they had the function of electing the eleven-member Black Affairs Council but had no other voting rights.

BAC was separatist in nature. Its primary objectives focused on black empowerment and self-determination as the means to achieve racial justice.

The 1968 General Assembly delegates voted that the UUA contribute $1 million to BAC in four annual payments. At the time I began my campaign for president, the UUA had already given $250 thousand to BAC.

In addition to the future funding of BAC, another campaign issue was whether the UUA should work with and contribute financially to Black and White Action (BAWA), a Unitarian Universalist organization that advocated blacks and whites working together to remedy racial ills (see the chapter "Associate Organizations"). The UUA board had recognized both BAC and BAWA. I felt that I understood the dynamics and rationale in each group and stated publicly that I could and would work with both. This approach was grounded in my belief that pluralism and voluntarism are inextricably woven into the fabric of our free religious movement.

The BAC-BAWA issue came to a head at the 1969 General Assembly. During the morning business session at which the seven presidential candidates presented their final campaign statements, a large number of BAC supporters walked out. The group adopted the name Moral Caucus and held meetings throughout the rest of the day in Arlington Street Church, where some speakers advocated forming a new denomination. The entire group returned to the assembly the next morning. Central to the walkout were whether the UUA would give money to both BAC and BAWA or solely to BAC and a demand that the UUA invest $6.5 million in black-controlled projects as reparations. BAC leaders stated earlier in the assembly that their organization would not accept any money from our Association if funds also were given to BAWA. Voting as a committee of the whole, the delegates approved giving funds only to BAC by a margin of twelve votes, 749 to 737, a decision the formal General Assembly later confirmed.

The assembly did not approve the demand that the UUA invest $6.5 million in black-controlled projects; instead the delegates passed a substitute motion that approved the UUA board's current policy concerning social responsibility and investments. In reflecting later on the events that occurred in our 1969 General Assembly, I was gratified that my supporters were ardent proponents of both BAC and BAWA. I believe that contributed significantly to providing a more solid foundation for making the difficult decisions and taking the necessary actions that lay ahead.

Those were some of the ingredients that created the circumstances with which the trustees and I struggled in ensuing months, culminating in severe staff reductions and program cuts (see the chapter "Financial Crisis and Organizational Changes"). Given our financial straits, the most troublesome issue for the new board was the amount to give BAC from the UUA budget for the current fiscal year that had begun July 1, 1969.

When the 1968 General Assembly voted that the UUA give BAC $1 million, the resolution specified that:

• In making its first annual $250-thousand contribution to BAC, the UUA would pay an initial $150-thousand amount no later than July 1, 1968.

• The UUA would raise the remaining $100 thousand during the eight-month period beginning that day.

• If the fundraising effort proved unsatisfactory, the UUA would make up the deficit.

• The above payment schedule would continue throughout the four-year period beginning July 1, 1968.

Under the UUA constitution and bylaws, the General Assembly did not have the power to appropriate funds or incur indebtedness but was legally restricted to making recommendations to the board, which had ultimate responsibility for allocating funds. The

UUA board had final authority regarding whether to take any of those actions voted by the General Assembly delegates.

In making payments to BAC in 1968, the UUA did not follow the schedule specified in the General Assembly resolution. Instead the board voted at its June 1968 meeting to pay $150 thousand on July 1, and the remaining $100 thousand in equal monthly installments without undertaking a fundraising effort. Those payments were for the 1968–1969 fiscal year. The board voted in the same meeting that it would make no commitments, express or implied, beyond the single year's contribution of $250 thousand. In a July 1968 letter explaining that vote, the UUA treasurer said it meant "there is no financial guarantee made to BAC beyond the fiscal year ending June 30, 1969."

However, after my election in the latter part of July 1969—and before the new board and I could consider steps to cope with the grim financial circumstances of the current fiscal year—the UUA treasurer from the outgoing administration paid $150 thousand to BAC. He made the payment on August 1, 1969, approximately ten days after my term as president officially began and before I arrived in Boston.

The circumstances associated with that payment are unsettling, to say the least, as there is no evidence the UUA treasurer had authority to make it. At its May 1969 meeting, the outgoing board adopted a 1969–1970 budget that the trustees clearly stated was subject to review by the incoming board. The departing board also instructed the treasurer that the 1969–1970 schedule for any payment to BAC was to begin on September 1—again with the provision that the schedule and amounts were subject to review by the new board.

In his letter of August 1 that conveyed the $150-thousand check to BAC, the treasurer stated that at a July 12 meeting the outgoing board had voted to change the payment date from September 1 to August 1. There is no evidence that a meeting of the UUA board occurred on July 12. The board meeting at the 1969 General Assembly was held on July 13, and the minutes of that meeting make no mention of a July 12 meeting, though they do report approving the minutes of the May board meeting and June executive committee meeting. The July 13 minutes of the outgoing board do not mention any change in the schedule of BAC payments, which the board had directed at its most recent meeting (May 16) were to begin on September 1 subject to reconsideration by the incoming board.

After reviewing the minutes of all board and executive committee meetings during that period, I can only conclude that either there was no proper authorization for the UUA treasurer to make the August 1 $150-thousand payment to BAC, or there was a meeting or action of the outgoing UUA board or executive committee that was kept out of the official UUA minutes. In an August 7 letter to the UUA treasurer acknowledging receipt of the $150-thousand check, the administrative secretary of BAC thanked him "for whatever role you personally played in changing the payment schedule."

As one of my recommendations to the board for action at its November 1969 meeting (see the chapter "Financial Crisis and Organizational Changes") I proposed that for 1969–1970 the Association pay $150 thousand to BAC, an amount it already had received, and that the UUA raise an additional $100 thousand for BAC from voluntary contributions, with cooperation from BUUC—the approach the 1968 General Assembly voted in Cleveland. The gist of my proposal was that we implement the same funding procedure written by BAC leaders in 1968 and approved by that General Assembly, including having the UUA make up the difference if our separate voluntary fundraising effort fell short.

However, the board voted at the November 1969 meeting to put $200 thousand in the 1969–1970 budget as the total UUA payment for that fiscal year, with the provision that if annual program fund contributions exceeded $1.3 million, up to $50 thousand of any such excess would also be paid to BAC. In addition, the trustees recorded their intent to budget sufficient annual amounts during the next three years to pay the remainder of the $1 million that the 1968 General Assembly recommended be given to BAC.

Knowing that the January 1970 board meeting agenda included a controversial proposal to restore the entire $250-thousand amount for BAC, the moderator and I decided to change the meeting location from UUA headquarters to the Statler Hotel, where there would be space in a huge room for the large number of observers expected. Despite there being more than ample space for everyone, BAC supporters insisted on standing in large numbers immediately behind and leaning over the shoulders of the seated board members, all the while engaging in intimidating and at times loud and insulting behavior.

I was saddened by the behavior of BAC supporters that day—and I was especially saddened by the deliberate disregard and disruption of free and open discussion that is essential to the democratic process in a free religious body. Their actions betrayed the ideals and principles of their denomination. I was gratified and touched when a few years ago one of them, who was a student in 1970, saw me in a church and apologized to me for his behavior in the Statler on that day thirty years earlier.

It is difficult for members of today's generation to envision the atmosphere of that period. Anti-institutionalism pervaded much of American society and our denomination. I believe the Vietnam War was a primary cause, and BAC events during those years certainly nourished it in our denomination. Confrontational politics were in vogue. Some ministers were publishing such sentiments as "UUA headquarters should be blown up" and "25 Beacon Street should be sunk in Boston Harbor." Microphones were seized during General Assembly sessions. One UUA board member en route to a General Assembly was heard to say that his mission was "to destroy the UUA." A BUUC leader once invaded my office while I was being interviewed by television reporters and commandeered the microphone while we were on camera.

Many were reluctant to give money to the UUA, primarily because of prior financial practices (see the chapter "Financial Crisis and Organizational Changes") and the various controversies churning our denomination, including congregational and UUA actions concerning the Vietnam War. The UUA Finance Committee reported other reasons as well: too much money was given to BAC; not enough money was given to BAC; BAWA was not funded; and the appropriation for Chicanos was cut. Another was the view of some donors that our newly instituted interdistrict representatives program ruined the concept of districts.

Despite the raucous protests at the January 1970 board meeting, which the *UU World* newspaper described as stormy, the UUA trustees did not change their November decision limiting our BAC contribution to $200 thousand for the current fiscal year. In their January meeting the trustees also reaffirmed the existing UUA policy concerning any fundraising undertaken by BAC, namely that BAC wasn't permitted to raise funds from Unitarian Universalist organizations, societies, or individuals other than assisting in the UUA annual program fund campaign. The Association had a longstanding policy that no funds from a UUA budget would be given to any group that engaged in competitive fundraising.

In response to the board's votes at the January meeting, BAC leaders publicly denounced the UUA as racist and threatened to disaffiliate from the Association because the UUA trustees did not approve the additional $50 thousand for BAC. BUUC leaders indicated they would approach individual congregations for financial support of BAC. I stated during a press conference, "In fairness it should be known that BAC was not 'first fired' by the UUA board in November. The board worked through an agonizing two days of meetings in reducing the overall budget by some $1 million, and voted the BAC $50-thousand reduction only as a last resort near the close of the meeting." I also reiterated my intention to continue my efforts at reconciliation.

BAC sent its statement of disaffiliation to the UUA board, while BUUC and BAC leaders appealed to individuals and congregations to cut their UUA annual program fund contribution by 25 percent and give it to BAC. BUUC and BAC also launched a fundraising campaign to raise $5 million from Unitarian Universalist individuals and congregations through the sale of

BAC bonds. BAC leaders declared they still expected the UUA to pay their organization the remainder of the $1-million figure voted by the 1968 General Assembly.

At its April 1970 meeting, the UUA board acknowledged receipt of the BAC statement of disaffiliation and voted that BAC was "hereby removed" from the official list of affiliated members. The trustees also approved a budget for the 1970–1971 fiscal year that included no funding for BAC because the organization had embarked on direct fundraising from Unitarian Universalist individuals and congregations; to fund BAC under those circumstances was contrary to longstanding UUA policy. An additional aspect was that though the 1969 General Assembly voted "that no funds be expended or distributed by the UUA from its budget to any organization funded by the UUA unless an annual audit by an independent, certified public accountant is supplied by said funded organization for the prior year's funds"—a policy the board affirmed in September 1969—no such audit had been received from BAC. The Association had paid BAC $250 thousand in 1968 and $200 thousand in 1969.

During the budget discussion in the April 1970 trustees' meeting, I noted that further cutbacks probably would be required in July, and stated, "I have to disagree that black empowerment stands above every other issue, because for the people charged with the life of this Association, I don't think black empowerment does stand above the issue of whether or not we are going to have a viable continental program." The majority sentiment of board members was that the Association's survival was the issue.

Racial Justice Fund

The business agendas of our 1970 and 1971 General Assemblies contained resolutions that would require the Association to contribute funds to BAC from the UUA annual budget, but the delegates did not approve them. The resolution on the agenda of the 1971 General Assembly in Washington called for 10 percent of the

UUA annual budget to be paid to BAC. On June 8, during a board discussion of the agenda item, I reported that I had made strenuous efforts to avoid confrontation about the issue in the impending General Assembly but had been unsuccessful. I called attention to the imminent danger of "everyone losing" from splitting the denomination and discouraging contributions. I said the budget couldn't be cut much further without endangering basic functions; if the current trend of annual program fund contributions did not improve, another drastic reorganization would be required.

Though the 1971 General Assembly defeated the initial BAC business resolution—as well as other attempts to have the UUA make payments from annual budgets to pay a full $1 million to BAC—the delegates eventually passed a substitute resolution by a vote of 512–387. The resolution stated, "Denominational division and polarization on the issue of how best to fight racism have gone on long enough, therefore the General Assembly desires a single, joint fundraising campaign to finance all Unitarian Universalist efforts (other than the Unitarian Universalist Service Committee) to achieve racial justice." The UUA board and administration were directed to "confer with BAC, BAWA, and all other interested parties to implement such united fundraising."

In the next edition of the *UU World* I wrote,

> The issue has not been whether the Black Affairs Council will be funded by our denomination. The issue has been how the Black Affairs Council will be supported—whether the funds will come from the UUA budget or from voluntary contributions by individuals and congregations throughout the denomination. The 1968 and 1969 general assemblies voted that the money was to come from the UUA budget, and $450 thousand was given directly to the Black Affairs Council from the UUA budget those two years. The 1970 and 1971 general assemblies voted that the money was not to come from the UUA budget but from voluntary contributions by congregations and individuals . . . .

I went on to state that the two main reasons the General Assemblies and UUA trustees voted to change the method of funding BAC were that we could not afford to cut further into UUA basic functions, and there was deeply divided opinion throughout our denomination regarding whether Unitarian Universalists wanted contributions from the UUA budget for furthering racial justice to go to BAC or BAWA. I said,

> We as a denomination are going through a process . . . of grappling with the problems of how, given the nature of our movement, we can apply our resources and energies effectively in the cause of black empowerment and racial justice and to combat racism. The process often is agonizing. . . .
>
> I have no doubt as to the sincerity and commitment and depth of that concern on the part of those persons engaged, though they may hold different views. . . . We in this free religious movement *will* do the best we can to apply our religion in our life, even though we surely do encounter difficulties. . . . Let us endeavor to find the means, through our differences, to do it *together*. I believe we can.

Immediately after the 1971 General Assembly passed the joint fundraising resolution, the board designated three trustees to investigate implementation. At the October board meeting, the three trustees reported their conclusion that a united fundraising effort for racial justice was "impractical" that year because the organizations involved would agree to participate only if certain conditions were met. The board responded by authorizing a hearing the following month to continue exploring how to implement the resolution. Seven UUA trustees conducted the November hearing, under instructions to report at the January board meeting; representatives from BAC, BAWA, the UUA, and the Unitarian Universalist Service Committee (UUSC) attended. During the October board meeting, the UUA administration put forth an alternative proposal that the trustees referred to the hearing: a proportional racial justice fund raised through the UUA fundraising department in an annual campaign parallel to our annual program fund.

In January 1972, the trustees who conducted the hearing submitted majority and minority recommendations to the board. The majority proposal guaranteed some funds from the UUA budget for both BAC and BAWA in 1972, and a total of $150 thousand the following year. The minority proposal established a voluntary fund that would attempt to raise $125 thousand in 1972 and $200 thousand the next year. The board defeated all the specific proposals, by a vote of 12 to 10 with two abstentions, and then adopted a resolution that declared, "Having heard the racial justice committee's report and received the specific proposals worked out by its members, the board regretfully concludes that none of them is fully acceptable to all the organizations most directly concerned, including the board itself." The board disbanded the committee and urged "individual Unitarian Universalists and congregations to give expression of their concern for black empowerment and racial justice by giving generous support to appropriate organizations."

Three months later, the board accepted $250 thousand as a designated gift from the Unitarian Universalist congregation in Plandome, New York, for the purpose of establishing a special fund to promote racial justice and combat racism. The grant was for the succeeding eighteen months and stipulated that $180 thousand be given to BAC, $45 thousand to BAWA, and $25 thousand to other projects to be determined. The six-member UUA administering committee reported that it "found both the BAC and BAWA philosophies to be respectable approaches to racial justice and not necessarily in competition."

When the initial grant expired in late 1973, the UUA board requested an additional amount to extend the racial justice fund through June 1974. The Plandome congregation approved an extension amount of $70 thousand. In January 1974, the administering committee reported that it would make no allocations to parties involved in the BUUC-BAC litigation (see the chapter "Black UU Caucus Court Proceedings"). At its March meeting, the committee made an allocation to BAWA, as well as to the UUA migrant ministry and inner-city child-care programs.

The administering committee also issued a statement containing the following recommendations, which the UUA trustees approved in April 1974:

> The committee feels frustrated by the lack of information and evaluation furnished by recipients, and feels it really cannot discharge its responsibility for the program under the present arrangement of predetermined grants to major agencies. The committee unanimously agrees that if the [grants] program is continued it should be handled on an individual program or project basis with the condition that future funding will not be forthcoming without adequate reporting and evaluation by recipients.

The committee said its funding policy "does not negate black empowerment, as evaluation criteria are to be established by [recipient] agencies, not the committee."

The committee also recommended that the racial justice fund be continued through May 1975, with one-third of the total amount to be allocated each six months. The committee stated that among its criteria for distributing funds were that a recipient program or project must promote racial justice and combat racism, and that no grants would be made to current program recipients until complete, satisfactory reports were received by the administering committee. The committee established specific rules for auditing, monitoring, reporting, and evaluating—and stated that BAC's reporting "does not show amounts expended, results obtained to date, or contact persons responsible for the program."

The UUA trustees approved a $100-thousand grant for the 1974–1975 fiscal year, allocated from a general block grant donated by the Plandome church (see the chapter "The Veatch Program and Holdeen Trusts"). As of May 1975, the administering committee for the racial justice fund had distributed $420 thousand. In addition to recipients noted earlier, allocations were made to the following types of programs: establishing small businesses, a mountain retreat for inner-city children, a North American Indian league, a video access center, Racial Justice Cadre, a district program to promote equal educational opportunity, a youth camp to develop leadership, minority elderly outreach, and a community law center.

BAC Bonds

BUUC and BAC embarked on direct fundraising from Unitarian Universalist individuals and congregations in early 1970. A subsequent BAC report stated that BAC had "become a full-fledged fundraising operation." In addition to receiving contributions that went directly to BAC in the usual fashion, the two groups launched a campaign to raise $5 million through the sale of BAC bonds. The proceeds were to be used for community-based black economic development programs. Issued in the name of the Black Affairs Council Investment Corporation (BIC), these bonds promised to annually pay buyers 5 percent of the original cost; at the end of ten years, the entire original purchase amount would be repaid to the buyer.

Based on the unanimous opinions of the UUA Investment Committee, Finance Committee, general counsel, and special financial advisor, the Association published its position regarding BAC bonds in the November 15, 1970, issue of the *UU World*. The prominently displayed announcement stated that "BAC bonds cannot be considered an investment. Any person or group purchasing BAC bonds must be prepared legally and personally to lose the money. No restricted funds may be used to purchase BAC bonds. The purchase of BAC bonds is to be considered a contribution or gift." The announcement also included a statement that the auditors' report for the UUA fiscal year 1969–1970 showed that our Association had no unrestricted capital funds remaining and owed some $550 thousand (see the chapter "Financial Crisis and Organizational Changes").

It was credibly reported in the early spring of 1971 that Unitarian Universalist churches, organizations, and individuals had pledged more than $1 million to purchase BAC bonds and that BAC intended to call for the money by April 20, 1971. For IRS purposes, BAC divided itself into three separate organizations: BAC, BIC, and BAC Action Council for political action. Another corporation also was created, Basic Venture Capital Corporation (BVCC). The board of the venture capital corporation was identical to the trustees of BAC, and the corporation obtained its money by selling its own stock to BIC, whose board also was identical to the trustees of BAC.

At its annual meeting in February 1972, BUUC voted to discontinue any further effort to seek funding from the UUA budget; the group also decided to seek associate membership in the UUA, which was the same type of membership held by organizations such as the Unitarian Universalist Women's Federation and Unitarian Universalist Service Committee. During the meeting, BUUC confirmed that its official political position was pan-African nationalism and reported that its members were active in many parts of the country in the political liberation councils of the Congress of African People.

Black UU Caucus Court Proceedings

DIVISIONS AMONG MEMBERS of Unitarian Universalist black power organizations came to a head amid legal proceedings that began in a Philadelphia courtroom in April 1973. The lengthy litigation included an alleged attempt by certain Black Affairs Council and Black Unitarian Universalist Caucus leaders to convert the BUUC organization into a black humanist entity that would drop the name Unitarian Universalist and have authority to conduct weddings and funerals. There also were allegations of mismanagement of BAC funds, and ultimately many churches, organizations, and individuals who had purchased BAC bonds lost substantial portions of their investment. The eight years of events involving BAC, from our 1968 General Assembly action to the 1976 culmination of legal proceedings, left many of us reflecting that it is not enough to want to do good, but to do good wisely.

At issue in the court action was the validity of the sixth annual BUUC meeting, held February 23 to 25, 1973. The dispute included BUUC, BAC, Black Affairs Council Investment Corporation (BIC), Basic Venture Capital Corporation (BVCC), Black Humanist Fellowship (BHF), and a number of individuals who were members, some of them officials, of BUUC and BAC when the annual meeting occurred. BUUC elected the BAC board, and BAC board members were the same people who constituted the boards of BIC and BVCC.

Ben Scott, treasurer of BAC at the time, brought the complaint in March 1973 on behalf of BUUC, BAC, BIC, BVCC, and several individuals. The defendants were Richard Traylor, who was administrative secretary of BAC when the meeting took place; Harold Wilson, chairman of BUUC; and BHF.

The complaint in *BUUC et al. v. Traylor et al.* alleged that Richard Traylor and Harold Wilson—in order to control BAC, BIC, BVCC, and all their assets—arranged to hold an illegal meeting of BUUC in Philadelphia on February 23. At this meeting, it was voted to change the name of BUUC to Black Humanist Fellowship; completely strike the words *Unitarian* and *Universalist* from the constitution; and set up a new operational structure that would include, among other features, incorporating local fellowships with the power to elect an elder who would have legal authority to perform marriages and funerals. The complaint also asserted that Harold Wilson appointed his own credentials committee; that Harold Wilson, Richard Traylor, and others suspended the BUUC constitution so no quorum was required; that unauthorized delegates were present and voted; and that all observers were prohibited from the meeting. The March suit contested actions taken during the February meeting on grounds that the meeting and its conduct violated the BUUC constitution.

On April 15, 1973, the *UU World* newspaper published a written statement by Dalmas Taylor, a member of BUUC, on behalf of the Ben Scott plaintiffs, alongside one by Richard Traylor for the defendants. BUUC members were "concerned about recent moves by a faction of leaders to turn BUUC into another denomination," declared Taylor, who went on to say,

> The separate church idea will end the relationship BUUC has had with the churches in the UUA. Churches and individuals have made available nearly a million dollars to corporations created by BUUC for the development of economic and societal institutions to increase the power of black communities for self-improvement. Eliminating

Unitarian Universalist identification and affiliation violates the assumptions its supporters have had that BUUC consists primarily of Unitarian Universalist congregants who are involved in the development of the black community. Members bringing the suit have a commitment to the black community and to all the congregations that have allocated their resources. Converting the Black Unitarian Universalist Caucus into a non-Unitarian Universalist religious group deprives us of an organization for which we labored for six years. Action was taken at a meeting that was contrived to ensure a favorable vote for the conversion by repeatedly violating the constitution. They have led their recruits to the religious group to believe that they can gain without effort, within a month, the benefits of the organizational efforts of the last six years.

Richard Traylor contended in his *UU World* statement that the February meeting regarding BUUC would not affect BAC or BIC:

BAC will still be an associate member of the UUA. Those favoring change felt BUUC had to move to its next level of growth. It was dead. Most of the folks working in it never were Unitarian Universalists anyway, so it was felt a large number of people who can be described as liberal religionists were being attracted to our movement. There are many black people who have been alienated from orthodox religion who are attracted to our programs—for the most part they are not joining any predominantly white institutions. . . . The people who did not favor the name change did not participate in the annual meeting, and having lost politically have decided to go into the courts. We will live with whatever decision the court makes.

The Philadelphia Court of Common Pleas entered a tentative decree in January 1974 that upheld the constitutional changes voted at the February 1973 meeting of BUUC. The court tentatively sanctioned the procedure of that meeting and approved the change in name from BUUC to Black Humanist Fellowship (BHF). If the decree were made final, BHF would be permitted to use the assets of BUUC and its affiliated corporations for the new purposes established at the February meeting. The tentative decree was scheduled to become final if no exceptions were filed within twenty days.

The BUUC plaintiffs filed exceptions, which meant a three-judge panel would conduct a trial-level review. The Philadelphia judge who had issued the tentative decree stated he would welcome the UUA as "friend of the court" during the review procedures. The UUA board accepted the judge's invitation, with the understanding that the Association's participation wasn't specifically on behalf of the plaintiffs or the defendants but intended solely to assist the court in establishing the facts and the law.

In September 1974, the three-judge panel conducted its review. BUUC had filed a petition to hold BHF in contempt of court, alleging that BHF had not maintained the status quo as previously ordered by the court, and thus had jeopardized the monies and assets of the BUUC plaintiffs. BUUC also asked for an accounting, and the court appointed an accountant to look into the matter.

The UUA board voted at its October 1975 meeting that information related to the BUUC-BHF court case should be forwarded to organizations and individuals who might have purchased BAC/BIC bonds. That information, from the audit of BIC for the fiscal year ending June 1973, included findings that the auditors were unable to complete their examination because of incomplete records and insufficient competent evidence. They could not express an opinion on financial statements and were unable to establish what happened to more than $90 thousand of proceeds from investments. They also were not satisfied with the starting point for their audit as furnished by BIC and noted that significant changes in BIC's financial position occurred after the end of the audited period.

The judge appointed another auditor to conduct further audits of BAC and BIC books. In September 1975, the auditor reported that he was still attempting to determine what happened to the assets. He stated, "There is vital information missing and not in the books, and there is a lack of complete continuity of the books." BUUC had moved in July 1975 to have Richard Traylor held in contempt of court, and three months later BHF moved to have Ben Scott adjudged in contempt of court as well. Information disclosed in the course of the Traylor depositions indicated that BIC derived about $850 thousand from selling bonds. Traylor acknowledged that he had spent at least $130 thousand of the money he controlled during a time when BIC had virtually no functioning program supporting minority small business. The total amount of assets remaining out of the $850 thousand was approximately $500 thousand. Also, there was a notice of mortgage foreclosure by a Philadelphia bank on a building owned by BIC, on which it owed some $50 thousand.

Because the Plandome congregation had contributed such a large sum to the UUA in 1972 to be given to BAC, the UUA board sent additional information to the congregation about an audit of BAC that Richard Traylor produced in court for the fiscal year ending June 1974. The documents stated that Traylor had verbally approved $70 thousand in expenses without providing "sufficient evidential matter" for the propriety of the expenses, and that BAC had advanced funds to BIC for administrative expenses without a vote authorizing such payment. BAC also contributed a substantial amount to BIC as an "investment," though the same individuals controlled both organizations. The auditors said they were not satisfied with the starting point for their audit as furnished by BAC and could not express an opinion on their overall statement because of such circumstances.

Subsequently, William Duffy, UUA counsel wrote a letter to all BIC bondholders noting that in late 1975 the court-appointed accountant filed a report on the handling of BIC monies between January 1973 and June 1975. The letter further explained that the accountant's report cited the deplorable condition of the books, the lack of systematic record keeping, and the fact that a complete set of books had not been kept from 1974 on. It was impossible for the accountant to use the books for his report, and for that reason he declined to give an opinion on the financial affairs of BIC.

Duffy observed that, despite those rather severe limitations, the accountant did present a detailed picture of Richard Traylor's handling of BIC funds during the period. Though BIC was virtually without a functioning program supporting minority small business, Traylor spent $94 thousand on the office operation. He also loaned $51 thousand to a corporation he helped found; the corporation later defaulted on the loan.

Though Ben Scott's handling of the BIC funds entrusted to him was to be the subject of the accountant's next report to the judge, Scott submitted an affidavit in December 1975 that set forth what funds he received and what happened to them. The UUA attorney in Philadelphia verified that Scott had produced the requisite securities, certificates of deposit, and bank passbooks to support the general outline and thrust of the accounting in his affidavits.

In his January 1976 letter to BIC bondholders, Duffy wrote that the "following conclusions can in my judgment be reasonably drawn about BIC's financial situation at this time: (a) the situation is steadily worsening; (b) of the approximately $840 thousand that BIC received, at least $232 thousand is gone." He also reported that the bank was moving to complete its mortgage foreclosure on the Philadelphia building owned by BIC.

Duffy informed the UUA board at its April 1976 meeting that the court's decision in the BUUC-BHF case was imminent, and that All Souls Church in Washington, a principal bondholder, had voted to take whatever action was necessary and appropriate to prevent further erosion of its investment in BIC bonds. Another principal bondholder, All Souls Church of Brooklyn, plus a number of other churches and individuals, joined with the Washington church and retained counsel to represent their interests in the Philadelphia litigation. Duffy also reported that the Philadelphia attorneys for each of the parties in the dispute had petitioned the court for payment of their fees from the remaining corporate funds.

On May 6, the judge ordered that neither plaintiffs nor defendants were to spend any corporate funds without specific court approval. Two weeks later, All Souls Church, acting for the majority of BIC bondholders, filed a petition in the Philadelphia court to have BIC dissolved and a receiver appointed to sell its assets and apply the proceeds as the court may order. The church said its interest in filing the petition was to "preserve its initial investment from mismanagement, internal conflict, and improper use; and to ensure that the remaining funds, loaned for the primary purpose of assisting minority enterprises, are not further eroded. . . ." The Washington congregation, which invested $162 thousand in BIC bonds, represented seven other Unitarian Universalist churches and numerous individuals who invested in BIC. (The $630 thousand that the UUA contributed to BAC was an outright gift, entirely apart from any money BAC/BIC obtained from selling BIC bonds.)

In the summer of 1976, the three-judge panel in Philadelphia ruled that the change of name from BUUC to BHF was invalid, and that all actions taken at the February 1973 annual meeting of BUUC were "null and invalid by reason of the absence" of a quorum. In its final decree, the court prohibited the defendants "from using in any manner whatsoever the name, designation, or words 'Black Humanist Fellowship' as successor or as related to Black Unitarian Universalist Caucus." The court noted that a separate judge had held extensive hearings on the issue of alleged mishandling, misapplication, and misappropriation of BUUC funds, and that a different jurisdiction had responsibility for those matters.

The court approved a settlement agreement that ended litigation in the BUUC-BHF case. The settlement provided that BIC bondholders who had claims to the remaining assets could decide on the disposition of their shares at a meeting to be held at All Souls Church in Washington on September 18, 1976. Signing the agreement were BUUC, BHF, BIC, the UUA as amicus, and BIC bondholders.

At the September 18 meeting, bondholders received ballots on which to convey their instructions to trustees of the funds. The options were: "give my share of the money to the proposal of the

BHF faction (Richard Traylor, Harold Wilson, et al.)," "give my share of the money to the proposal of the BUUC faction (Ben Scott, et al.)," "return my share of the money to me." Some two-dozen BIC bondholders were present to hear the proposals on which to base their decisions. Ballots and pertinent written material were mailed to bondholders who were not present.

Prior to the meeting, the BHF faction sent bondholders a letter signed by Hayward Henry, Richard Traylor, Harold Wilson, and others that said in part,

> We will not present a proposal on September 18. . . . We have concluded that the remaining assets of BIC should be used to redeem the bonds to the extent the assets will allow. . . . We feel that there are several reason why the BIC experiment with Unitarian Universalists should be ended: (1) The five years that are now left before the bonds are due to be repaid does not represent a sufficient amount of time for the development of any businesses. (The original ten years was even cutting it short.) (2) The whole national climate is one of reaction and conservatism which does not produce support from government nor most of the private sector except for programs of the most classical and conservative constructs. (3) Much of what we projected as BIC's potential depended upon a strong BAC administrative operation. This does not now exist and has not existed since November 1974.

The BHF letter said the signers believed racism played a major role in the way the litigation proceeded and that "our administrative operation died despite the tremendous effort we expended to keep it alive."

The BUUC faction made a presentation to the bondholders on behalf of Ben Scott and others, all of whom were trustees of BAC and members of the investment council of BIC. The written statement traced the history of the litigation and said,

> In due time the merits of the case were argued before the court. . . . On June 3, 1976, the court *en banc* ruled basically in

favor of the plaintiffs . . . By that time all of the assets which had been held by the defendants (Richard Traylor et al.), including at least $165 thousand in bond proceeds, had been dissipated and the only sound assets of the Black Affairs Council Investment Corporation (BIC) which remained were those managed by the treasurer, Benjamin F. Scott. . . . This fund started at $499.6 thousand and stands now at about $520 thousand. . . .

The BUUC faction's proposed plan for managing funds left with BIC involved administering them the same way funds held by Ben Scott had been managed: buying Government National Mortgage Association securities and investing the monthly proceeds in two black-controlled Chicago banks. Any assets currently held by the defendants (Richard Traylor et al.) would be liquidated and applied against outstanding liabilities. BIC would have no salaried employees and would not pay for services rendered by BAC, BUUC, or their affiliates.

In an oral portion of the presentation, Ben Scott said that the funds bondholders chose to leave with BIC would be used to back residential mortgage loans in minority areas, and that the plan, if successful, would permit substantial recovery of prior investment losses by the time most bonds matured in 1981. He also reported that BVCC, which was formed to be a minority-enterprise, small-business investment corporation, would be activated.

The initial distribution of funds to BIC bondholders was made in March 1977, with a small final distribution anticipated later in the year. Of 181 total bondholders, checks were mailed to 103 people who voted to have their shares of the remaining BIC assets returned to them; they received 55 percent of the amount they had originally paid, plus a final distribution of up to 5 percent. Those 103 bondholders represented about 45 percent of the total amount of BIC bonds. Holders of the remaining 55 percent of the total amount voted to leave their shares invested under the control of Ben Scott, the BIC treasurer.

In contemplating the totality of events known as the BAC controversy in our denomination, my feelings are primarily sadness and regret—sadness and regret about what could have been and what was and is the expenditure of an enormous amount of energy, idealism, and resources, both human and financial.

Many have pondered the factors that may have caused people to commit so readily to placing such a large amount of money in the hands of BAC leaders. In conversations about the era, some of the questions I have heard expressed are: Was the strong idealism that is characteristic of most Unitarian Universalists part of the problem? Was it their deep-seated devotion to the grandest principles in our long tradition of a prophetic church? Their profound commitment to social reform as a religious imperative? Did it make people feel good—regardless of not knowing where the money was going, only that it was being put into the hands of black persons? How extensive a factor was "white guilt"? How significant was the element of trust? To what extent were people misled by leaders, white or black? Was it a matter of some General Assembly delegates finding it easy to vote to give away money they believed wasn't coming from their own pockets? Was it a classic instance of a well-organized special-purpose organization learning to manipulate our General Assembly machinery? Did "black empowerment" have elements of a rigid theology that, once embraced, could not be deviated from?

Animosities and divisions regarding the BAC issue continued through the years of my presidency. They began to abate about two years before the end of my second term, but when I left office in 1977, bitterness and disagreement continued to pervade our denomination concerning the best approach to remedying our racial ills.

Throughout those tumultuous years of controversy, I tried to do what I had stated in my campaign literature I would do. I supported the pluralism of the honestly held divergent beliefs of those who advocated the "blacks only" position, as well as those who favored the "blacks and whites" approach. I was aware that I had been elected president of the entire denomination—not of one faction or one cause or one region, but of all our congregations and members.

Keeping in mind that the primary purpose of the UUA is to serve the basic needs of congregations, I tried to preserve the programs that were essential to fulfilling that purpose. I cannot emphasize strongly enough that the strength of our religious movement resides in the day-to-day lives of our local members and the professional leaders of our congregations. I was determined to work through all the difficulties we encountered, to keep in mind the long-term health of our denomination, to keep the UUA on a sound financial basis, and to uphold the ideals of our Unitarian Universalist movement.

I have been told there are some people today who are still bitter about how BAC was funded. They say they were defeated in their effort to prevent our denomination from turning its back on black people. I say that what was defeated was the particular tactic they advocated for our denomination to employ in combating racial injustice. The UUA chose to follow a different approach in trying to help the cause of blacks: one that was within its means and in accord with the pluralism that is essential in our democratic denomination; one that resulted in our denomination giving in excess of $1.5 million to blacks-only organizations and programs as well as more than an additional $220 thousand to blacks-and-whites programs. BAC received $630 thousand directly from the UUA.

I disagree with those who say today that our denomination turned its back on black people in 1969, 1970, and 1971. The particular tactic they advocated at that time was thoroughly considered by the UUA but not followed exclusively. Our denomination continued to work steadily for the cause of racial justice and empowering blacks, through its own endeavors and by financing outside organizations and programs.

It was an agonizing period, as we grappled with the problems of how to apply our resources and energies effectively in the cause of racial justice and to combat racism. All during that era, I did not doubt the commitment and depth of concern on the part of the individual Unitarian Universalists actively engaged in those causes, though they held opposing viewpoints.

The overriding issue in the BAC controversy wasn't whether our denomination would provide funding to combat racial injustice, or even whether it would give money to BAC. The paramount issue was whether to perilously weaken core services to our congregations in order to give a very large amount of money to a single cause. The circumstances were intensified by deep division over whether BAC was the best and only approach for furthering racial justice.

During that period, a number of my friends were dedicated primarily to helping promote black empowerment. Though I had spent years of my life in the South and in the North working for the cause of racial justice, I was dedicated primarily to preserving our Unitarian Universalist denomination as an effective movement.

UUA moderator Joseph Fisher expressed one of my recurring thoughts about those years in an address three months before our terms ended. Noting that in regard to social action, "our appetites have sometimes outrun our resources," he continued, "As always, the problem of free men and women is to exercise their freedom wisely and responsibly." He observed that this freedom involves "excruciating choices that test a person's religion and common sense. In these choices and how we make them is the essence of social responsibility."

Second-Term Considerations

I recall a lonely meeting with Joseph Fisher at my office on a rainy Sunday afternoon in 1972, several months before our concurrent four-year terms ended. I use the word lonely though two of us were present; I believe we both felt that during those difficult decades no one else was fully aware of the personal conflict and fatigue we often experienced.

The purpose of our meeting was to discuss running for a final four-year term ending in 1977. I sensed that neither of us relished the prospect of spending four more years enduring the type of experiences that had characterized the preceding seven years for him, and nearly four for me. Toward the end of our conversation, Joe stated that if we both weren't candidates in the upcoming election, the denomination would be split as it was in the period from 1968 to 1971; the result would be the reopening of old wounds and intense conflict throughout our denomination.

I didn't disagree with his analysis. We decided to run for office and were unopposed.

Contrast in General Assemblies

The 1972 and 1973 General Assemblies were markedly different in tenor and ambiance from those of the preceding three years. Apparently the decisive votes of our 1970 and 1971 General Assemblies, precluding the use of UUA annual budgets to fund BAC, had eased the atmosphere of tension and conflict that permeated earlier assemblies. The lead *UU World* article of June 15, 1973, reported that the general feeling during the 1972 General Assembly in Dallas was: "There's too much unfinished business in the world to waste our energies on abrasive infighting. Let's get together and get on with the job." The writer went on to observe that the 1973 General Assembly in Toronto "was a reflection of that attitude."

Almost every event at the Toronto assembly set new attendance records. The morning worship services experienced heavy turnouts, and dancing sessions sponsored by BAWA and LRY attracted hundreds of participants. Delegates passed amendments removing gender discrimination in UUA bylaws, defeated the recurrent effort to hold General Assemblies biennially instead of annually, passed a resolution urging the UUA board to select college campuses or other non-hotel sites for future General Assemblies, and reelected Joseph Fisher and me for four additional years.

Hopefully, no other UUA president will have an experience similar to the earlier portion of my time in office. It's up to General Assembly delegates and congregations and individual members throughout our denomination to assure that it doesn't happen—

not just for the sake of the woman or man who is elected president but for our denomination as a whole. To them I would say: Act for the present, but care for the future.

Publishing

IN MY 1969 CAMPAIGN brochure, I had named improved communication as an essential goal of my presidency. I pointed out that there was an information blockage and observed that we had no common experience as individuals in our denomination. Because publishing has always been at the heart of our Unitarian and Universalist denominations—from pamphlets, books, journals, and worship materials to religious education curricula and the Pentagon Papers—I proposed that a newspaper in all our homes would be a great aid, particularly if much space were devoted to a vigorous exchange of opinion. Thus we established the *UU World* as the journal of the UUA, published twice each month during most months, once a month in others, and mailed free of charge to the home of every contributing member in every congregation that would send us the names and addresses. Our objective was to create a medium for timely, two-way communication between all the people in our congregations, UUA headquarters, and continental organizations. *UUA Now*, the denominational magazine the *UU World* replaced, had a circulation of approximately seven thousand. It was largely a one-way communication, and its news pieces were very out of date by the time subscribers read them.

From the moment I first mentioned the need for such a denominational journal, there were those who declared it to be an impossible objective. The reasons most frequently cited were the high costs of publication and distribution and—in light of the sense of mistrust that existed in much of the denomination—the reluctance of congregations to share their lists of contributing members with UUA headquarters. In the space of one month, however, congregations sent us the addresses of sixty thousand contributing households to receive the first issue of *UU World*. Two weeks later, the number had risen to seventy-eight thousand and after another six weeks the circulation reached ninety-five thousand. *UU World* began publication March 1, 1970, and by 1971 the newspaper was mailed regularly to more than 110 thousand families.

The difference in cost for the UUA to publish and distribute the newspaper was made up primarily from discontinuing the monthly information packet, eliminating nearly all additional general mailings from headquarters, and reducing other information programs. The total amount in the new UUA annual budget for communications, including the newspaper, was $70 thousand less than was spent the previous year.

It is difficult to convey the nature of the *UU World* newspaper in a few words. Every issue contained a large and vigorous letters-to-the editor section. There were numerous guest editorials and in-depth articles covering a wide range of subjects that included theology, history, and philosophy, as well as local, regional, national, international, and ecumenical topics. The publication regularly included extensive coverage of local congregations, as well as stories about individual Unitarian Universalists; denominational organizations across the continent; and geographically widespread social action. Ministers and lay members contributed expressions of faith, in addition to their opinions concerning current news topics. Book reviews and poetry were regular features. The *UU World* was a rich store of people, congregations, opinions, organizations, events, and numerous other elements of our communal life.

From its inception, the newspaper gave regular space to associated organizations and UUA departments, via columns authored

by correspondents who were selected by each of two dozen participating organizations and six departments. Many of those groups also placed advertisements, some as long as several pages, to describe their programs, present their views, and communicate with their members as well as others in Unitarian Universalist congregations.
In recently reading issues of *UU World* from 1970 to 1977, I was impressed by the dynamism, thought, interchange, and enthusiasm for liberal religious ideals they evidence. I found myself moved—not only by the intellectual, emotional, and theological exchange that was manifest—but by congregations and individuals who, even amid the controversies and troubles in our religious movement, put those ideals and values into practice in their daily lives.

Doris Pullen was named editor-in-chief of the *UU World* in early 1972. A few months later, she was appointed director of the UUA publications department, retaining her responsibilities as editor-in-chief of the newspaper. In June 1975, she became director and editor-in-chief of the Department of Communications and Development. Ms. Pullen was the first woman to be appointed a department director in our Association and the first female member of the UUA executive staff.

Sexuality Education

I was especially pleased by two projects that were realized during the time I was president, as they originated while I was a member and then chairman of the Advisory Committee for the UUA Division of Education from 1964 to 1969. One was the program for certifying professional directors of religious education (see the chapter "Professional Religious Leadership"), and the other a religious education curriculum unit titled *About Your Sexuality*.

In November 1967, the UUA Division of Education reported to the board that the most important development in its work during the past year "was centered around the creating of new religious education curricula that reflected the latest insights of child research and educational psychology. We were not only aware of the revolution taking place in the field of education, but sensitive to the needs of our growing movement for fresh and more imaginative programs." Some of the new curriculum units the UUA began developing during that period took the form of printed materials and a multimedia kit that included filmstrips and audiotapes.

One kit was the sexuality education curriculum *About Your Sexuality*, developed for use with junior-high-age students. Several years earlier, as minister of the First Unitarian Church in Rochester, New York, I was approached by a physician who was a member of the congregation and the mother of two children. She believed there was a strong need for sexuality education in our church, especially at the junior-high level, and asked if I would approve her teaming with a male teacher to create and conduct a course as part of our education program. I expressed my support, and the classes became a regular addition to the life of the congregation. I subsequently told the UUA advisory committee of the successful experiment in Rochester and encouraged the development of a sexuality education curriculum unit for our Association.

In the fall of 1969, the UUA Department of Education was field testing the *About Your Sexuality* curriculum. One morning, our curriculum editor informed me that the junior-high students who participated in the testing had expressed strong objections to the use of stick figures in the filmstrips to depict human beings. He requested my authorization to replace the stick figures with color photographs of professional models, and I agreed. On another occasion, the editor advised me that the preliminary version of *About Your Sexuality* was being criticized because it presented a heterosexual orientation only. He sought my consent to include information about gay and lesbian sexual orientations. I approved the proposed change.

Because our curriculum's forthright text and photographs might be interpreted as violating obscenity laws, the UUA board voted in April 1971 to delay distribution pending an initial report from UUA counsel and, if necessary, to hold a special meeting to review the content of the unit. During the discussion, a board member stated, "We are going to have to stand up straight and do some pioneering. We will have to deal with the question of leadership to the point of being sued if necessary."

The UUA published *About Your Sexuality* in the fall of 1971. The stated goal of the team that developed the curriculum was to "help young people explore according to their interest the facts, feelings, attitudes, and values they must take into consideration in order to understand their own sexuality and to be responsible decision makers in this area of their lives." The four specific objectives of the curriculum were to help young people get accurate information, develop communication skills in the subject of human sexuality, build attitudes and values, and make responsible decisions.

In contrast to the absence of visual aids in most sexuality education materials of the day, the unit included filmstrips that contained photographs of male and female professional models. Its editors pointed out that visual aids had become an integral part of the formal educational process in every subject except sexuality, and that esthetically presented visual materials clarified areas of sexuality that traditionally had been shrouded in mystery. The curriculum also included poetry and music about love, as well as booklets containing individual questionnaires for students. The content of the unit encompassed a range of sexuality, from exclusively heterosexual to exclusively homosexual. *About Your Sexuality* was taught by carefully selected teams trained in intensive workshops under expert leaders. Any congregation wishing to use the curriculum was required to agree that the course would be taught only by such qualified teachers.

Newsweek and the *New York Times* were among the publications that printed articles about the new UUA sexuality curriculum. In early 1972, a county district attorney threatened to prosecute the Unitarian Church West of Brookfield, Wisconsin, for violating state obscenity laws unless the teaching materials were cleared with him in advance of their use. The church proceeded to offer the course to its junior-high-age students without acceding to the district attorney's demands and sought a preliminary injunction in federal court to prevent his interference. Less than two days before the course was scheduled to begin, a federal judge in Milwaukee upheld the church's legal right to teach it. The judge said,

> The issue in this case is twofold. The first aspect is whether churches or parents in teaching their children about sex can be limited to silence and cryptic admonitions, or whether they can instead engage in a candid conversation. . . . The second aspect is whether the state in an effort to suppress obscenity can pursue a course which chills the exercise of freedom of religion, freedom of parents to educate their children, freedom of speech—three rights which are so synonymous with the United States that it is impossible to conceive of our nation without them.

The county district attorney appealed the judge's decision to the federal appeals court in Chicago, which in March 1973 upheld the right of the Wisconsin church to teach *About Your Sexuality*. The appeals court affirmed the entire decision of the Milwaukee judge in a ruling described as "a very strong victory for the local church and the UUA." The county district attorney responded by filing a petition for review in the U.S. Supreme Court; the UUA continued its legal assistance to the congregation by filing an amicus brief opposing the district attorney's petition. In 1974, the Supreme Court sent the case back to the lower courts, saying a declaratory judgment rather than an injunction should have been issued. The entire matter came to a conclusion in the spring of 1975, with the election of a new county district attorney who agreed to end all legal action concerning the *About Your Sexuality* course.

In 1972, the UUA Department of Education arranged with Dr. Dorothy Bennett to evaluate the *About Your Sexuality* curriculum by developing a research program to answer questions about what happened to young people who participated in the course. A school psychologist with special training in testing, Bennett developed and tested a research questionnaire for use by congregations, with the understanding that those completing the questionnaire would remain anonymous. The questionnaire was also given to young people who did not participate in the program and was administered twice to both groups with an interval of six months. The influence of *About Your Sexuality* spread beyond our denomination. For example, when the Southeast Wisconsin Unitarian Universalist Council offered training for teachers of the course, fewer than half the attendees were Unitarian Universalists. Of the thirty-two participants, nineteen were from university faculties, social work agencies, public schools, and church organizations affiliated with other denominations. The other thirteen were from Unitarian Universalist churches in Wisconsin and Illinois.

By 1973, *About Your Sexuality* was being used by family planning agencies, private and public schools, hotlines, prisons, schools for the deaf, and others. The British Broadcasting Corporation (BBC) sought information regarding the curriculum for two television projects, and a BBC representative visited UUA headquarters to learn about it; the course had been recommended to her by staff members of the Kinsey Institute, as well as by others engaged in sexuality research and evaluation. A number of universities also requested information and assistance in presenting the course.

An interesting sidelight occurred in the fall of 1973, when British customs authorities impounded *About Your Sexuality* filmstrips on grounds they were indecent. The curriculum kit was being sent to the BBC to be used in two television projects, one on sex education for parents and the other on human sexuality. Two filmstrips were seized under a law enacted in 1876. Given four weeks to appeal the government's action, the BBC elected not to contest the impoundment.

Beacon Press

Founded in 1854, Beacon Press is an independent, nonprofit publisher of serious nonfiction and fiction. Institutionally, it is a de-

partment of the UUA, and its mission is to fulfill the principles
and ideals of our Association, with special emphasis on promoting the values of freedom of speech and thought, religious pluralism, antiracism, diversity, and respect for our environment.

In the early 1970s, UUA trustees appointed the Beacon Press
director and board. The UUA president was an ex officio board
member; the director of the Press was a member of the UUA executive staff and attended all our weekly and special meetings. The
UUA covered the total amount of Beacon's annual losses and provided the buildings and infrastructure for their office operations.
Each year, the director and board of the press attempted as a minimum to break even financially, but that never happened when I
was president.

Given those circumstances, in combination with the critical
UUA financial condition (see the chapter "Financial Crisis and
Organizational Changes"), one can understand why there were
efforts to change some aspects of the joint arrangement. In late
1969 and early 1970, I met with a working group over a period of
weeks to explore possible changes that would benefit both Beacon
Press and the UUA. The substance of the ensuing proposal was
that the press would have the same relationship to the UUA as the
successful Church of the Larger Fellowship model (see the chapters "Financial Crisis and Organizational Changes" and "UUA
Offices") and similar to the Unitarian Universalist Service
Committee: Beacon Press would choose its own director and
board members, raise its own funds independent of the UUA, and
remain part of our Association as an associate member; the UUA
would continue to provide financial support until Beacon
achieved a sound footing. However, a majority of the Beacon Press
board declined to approve the proposal.

Later in 1970, the UUA board appointed a special committee
to explore ways to ease the financial difficulties associated with
Beacon. During the previous eight years, the average amount of
annual UUA support for the press had been $90 thousand plus an
additional $30 thousand for office space, heat, light, and personnel

benefits, the equivalent of more than $775 thousand a year today. The press had been growing, and its annual budget at that point was roughly the size of the UUA budget. To continue at its current level of nonprofit publishing, Beacon needed to look elsewhere for financial support; owing to the financial developments of recent years, the UUA had no unrestricted funds remaining from which to support Beacon. In 1972, the UUA board acted on the special committee's recommendations and made Beacon Press a financially self-controlled corporation that remained a department of the UUA. The new arrangement significantly increased the degree of independence for Beacon Press; it could engage in its own fundraising and financing operations, and its director was responsible solely to the Beacon board, which had responsibility for the overall policy and direction of the press. However, the UUA trustees retained the authority to appoint the Beacon Press board.

The UUA trustees voted to guarantee a $200-thousand bank loan to Beacon Press in October 1972 and three months later approved an extension. In the spring of 1973, Beacon launched a fundraising campaign to create a permanent capital fund, with the hope that its earned income would replace the former UUA subsidy. The director of the press described its situation as "operating a $1.5-million business with no working capital." He also cited a report from an external consultant that, despite the risky nature of its publishing program, Beacon Press earned through book sales a significantly higher portion of its operating budget than did the average university press.

The Beacon board chairman reported to the UUA trustees at their October 1973 meeting that, as in the past, the press was experiencing two continuing problems: funding the annual deficit of its overall operations and securing sufficient working capital. He said the press needed a bank loan of $75 thousand for not more than ninety days, which the UUA board voted to guarantee. That fall Beacon announced an agreement whereby Harper & Row would warehouse its books, with Harper & Row sales staff representing Beacon in college, trade, and religious bookstores. In 1974, the

UUA board authorized the treasurer to guarantee bank loans for Beacon Press not to exceed a total of $75 thousand at any one time.

By early 1975, it was obvious that the 1972 financial and organizational arrangement had not succeeded in alleviating Beacon's intrinsic problems. The UUA board took several actions with the proviso that Beacon Press would no longer engage in independent fundraising and would make every effort to be self-sustaining: UUA trustees voted to establish a reserve fund for Beacon's operations; retain the Beacon Press Permanent Fund, which had been set up to accept capital gifts designated for the Press; give Beacon $102 thousand in immediate aid; and assist the Press with special financial needs that might arise from time to time in the future. During subsequent years, the UUA board continued to approve a revolving $100-thousand bank-loan guarantee. Another major change in Beacon Press operations occurred in 1975 when it created Skinner House Books to separate Unitarian Universalist denominational publishing from Beacon's general trade publishing. The Association continues to own both publishing houses today.

As Gobin Stair, director of Beacon Press, said during the Pentagon Papers episode, "The dialogue of publishing is for us similar to the dialogue of the pulpit." He said Beacon Press "is intended as a press of principle, able to suggest the meaning, the importance, and the priorities of the life questions that surround us constantly. Such a press is a religious press, bound into, participating in, and responsive to the culture" in which we find ourselves. As I recently reviewed the list of authors and books published by Beacon during the eight years I was UUA president, it is clear they were fulfilling that purpose enunciated by Gobin— not only for our denomination but also for the larger society.

Pentagon Papers

IN 1967, SECRETARY OF DEFENSE Robert McNamara ordered a secret study of American decision making in regard to the Vietnam War. The report was completed in early 1969 and became known as the Pentagon Papers. Two copies of the study were sent to the Rand Corporation, where Daniel Ellsberg and Anthony Russo ultimately made another copy, most of which Ellsberg leaked to the *New York Times* in 1971.

On June 13 of that year, the newspaper published its first article containing excerpts and summaries from the Pentagon Papers, and a few days later the *Washington Post* followed suit. The government immediately sought court injunctions to prevent any further publication. On June 30, after hearing appeals from conflicting lower court decisions, the U.S. Supreme Court ruled that the *New York Times* and other newspapers could not be precensored but left the door open for prosecution after publication of such articles. During a June 29 meeting of his Subcommittee on Building and Grounds, Senator Mike Gravel entered the Pentagon Papers into its records, and then released the complete text of some seven thousand typewritten pages to the press. The Associated Press ran approximately eighty thousand words on its Teletype that night, and portions were printed in numerous daily newspapers.

That was when the Pentagon Papers were made public. On July 8, 1971, Bantam Books published *The New York Times Edition of the Pentagon Papers* as a one-volume paperback, a synopsis of the narrative plus a number of the documents. Beacon Press was approached on July 26 as the possible publisher of a full version of the Pentagon Papers.

A few days later, the director of Beacon Press, Gobin Stair, requested my approval for Beacon Press to publish the Pentagon Papers. He told me that thirty-five other publishers had declined to publish them, though one had published limited excerpts. Gobin estimated that our cost to publish them would be $50 thousand, a huge expense given our financial condition at that time. I gave my approval and on August 17 Beacon Press publicly announced it would publish the Senator Gravel edition of the Pentagon Papers.

At the press conference announcing the scheduled publication, editor-in-chief Arnold Tovell reported that the edition would be a four-volume set of three thousand pages, and that Beacon Press would release 20 thousand copies in October. He said, "We believe [these volumes] will be a basic reference which will be analyzed and pondered for decades as citizens, scholars, and students try to unravel exactly how a well-meaning nation could have committed such a colossal blunder in its foreign affairs." Senator Gravel stated, "The Pentagon Papers show that we have created, in the last quarter-century, a new culture, protected from the influences of American life by the shield of secrecy."

On October 22, 1971, Beacon Press published *The Senator Gravel Edition of the Pentagon Papers—The Defense Department History of United States Decision Making on Vietnam*, which included the narrative and 265 documents. In the introduction, Senator Gravel wrote that had the true facts been known by the American people "the war would long ago have ended, and the needless deaths of hundreds of thousands of Americans and Vietnamese would have been averted. This is the great lesson of the Pentagon Papers."

Three significant events occurred between the August 17 announcement and October 22 publication: The Defense Department published its own version of the Pentagon Papers by simply reproducing the sometimes illegible manuscript, without consecutive page numbers for reference and with vital portions missing; two agents from the Defense Department visited Gobin Stair at his office, an experience Gobin described as ominous and intimidating; and Gobin reported that President Nixon telephoned him and, after noting what a nice person Gobin was, said he was sure Gobin did not want to get into any trouble by publishing the Pentagon Papers.

On a morning in early November 1971, the UUA treasurer came into my office and informed me that a vice president of New England Merchants Bank had just telephoned to tell him that FBI agents had been working at the bank for the past seven days. The agents were acting secretly under a subpoena from the federal grand jury that called for copies of all UUA financial records, including every check written and every check deposited in UUA accounts over a period of four-and-a-half months. Effectively the subpoena demanded copies of thousands of checks, including those of all individuals who contributed to the UUA.

Senator Gravel immediately brought contempt proceedings against the government on grounds of senatorial immunity and succeeded in halting the FBI examination of our bank records until the Appeals Court could rule on the immunity issue. In December, I instructed UUA counsel to be ready to resist in court any efforts by the FBI or grand jury to resume their investigation of our bank records. The court decision regarding Gravel's immunity was expected within a few days, at which time the grand jury probably would be free to continue its investigation.

The court issued its decision on January 7, 1972: The senator had immunity but it did not extend to parties such as Beacon Press and the UUA who republished the Pentagon Papers that he made public. Though the court had extended its stay of the investigation for an additional three weeks to permit appeals to the

Supreme Court, the FBI informed our bank on January 10 that the grand jury subpoena of all UUA bank records had been reissued.

The UUA filed suit in federal court the next day against the FBI, Justice Department, and grand jury, seeking to halt the investigation. In our complaint, we emphasized the grounds of religious freedom and freedom of association, as well as freedom of the press. At 1:30 that afternoon, I held a press conference at UUA headquarters to announce our court action. During this session, FBI agents served subpoenas on Gobin Stair, summoning him to appear before the grand jury with all Pentagon Papers records. However, as the press conference continued, the agents abruptly returned to Gobin's office and retrieved his subpoenas. Meanwhile, the identical scenario was occurring on the third floor of our UUA headquarters building: FBI agents delivered subpoenas to the UUA treasurer but quickly returned and recovered them and departed by the back stairway before our press conference ended.

In filing suit to halt the investigation, UUA attorneys included with their formal complaint my personal affidavit containing the following statements:

> At the core of the Unitarian and Universalist religion are freedom of conscience, individual freedom of belief, and the application of one's religion in daily actions of public and private nature. Our churches are noncreedal. Our denomination is a voluntary association of congregations.
>
> Beacon Press is the publishing operation of our Association. Beacon Press publishes books in such areas as religious education, religious history, religious thought, worship, contemporary religion, Unitarianism and Universalism, and hymnals—as well as world affairs, philosophy, ethics, child guidance, education, anthropology, poetry, and the fine arts. Beacon Press is a nonprofit tax-exempt publishing operation which is not incorporated and is not a separate entity. In carrying out the practice of the Unitarian Universalist religion, which emphasizes that participation in matters of social concern and working to improve the con-

dition of human beings is as much a part of one's religion as is theology, Beacon Press has published books of a controversial nature which other publishers are unwilling to publish. The operating budget of the Association for the current fiscal year is $1,730,000. Approximately two-thirds of the operating budget is received from the current contributions of congregations and individual donors. Nearly all the remaining one-third is derived from income on invested funds received from past donations.

Unless a donor indicates otherwise, it is and has been our uniform practice not to disclose the identity of individual donors, and many of our donors rely upon our continuing that practice. Some of our donors specify that their identity as donors be kept confidential. Disclosure to a federal grand jury and to government attorneys and investigators working with them of the identity of those donors and the amounts they have contributed would result in the breach of anonymity which not only protects them but promotes confidence in prospective donors. Such disclosures would have an adverse effect upon the fundraising on which our Association depends for its existence and programs. . . .

Also, I believe that a broad investigation which involves the FBI, grand jury, and Justice Department probing into the Association's affairs would adversely affect our fundraising because of the possible connotation of wrongdoing and criminality often associated with those agencies in people's minds.

Such an investigation also has the effect of intimidating present and prospective members of our denomination and interferes with their rights to freedom of association. Our existence and health are dependent on our being able to keep present members and add new ones. The broad investigation contemplated here would have an adverse effect upon the number of and rate of new members joining our denomination.

I object to any investigation under which the government would gain access to records which show in minute detail the receipts and expenditures of the Association for a period extending for 4 1/2 months. . . . The broad investigation referred to and described in the Complaint to which this affidavit is attached violates the religious freedom guaranteed by the First Amendment to the United States Constitution and constitutes an unwarranted intrusion by the government into the affairs of a religious denomination.

Throughout its history the Association has played an active role in controversial causes. Such causes in modern time include early and continuing opposition to the war in Vietnam, the repeal of antiabortion statutes, and support of practical steps to achieve racial justice. These efforts and many like them are part of the expression and practice of the Unitarian Universalist religion.

I believe that such broad access and investigation would subject our denomination to governmental intimidation and harassment, repress legitimate dissent, and infringe upon the religious freedom and the freedom of the press guaranteed by the First Amendment of the United States Constitution.

Immediately after our suit was filed, I sent a letter to forty religious leaders in which I informed them of the recent events and wrote, "The government's actions forebode intimidation of all religious bodies. An individual citizen's right to join and support a religious organization should not be subject to government investigation." The resulting strong expressions of support were gratifying. A joint statement issued by the executive secretaries of the National Council of Churches and the Synagogue Council of America criticized the government's actions as having "a chilling effect on the free exercise of religion." They said, "Whenever the religious liberty of one religious group is limited, all religious groups—and all citizens—are threatened thereby. . . . We reject the contention that the government is dealing not with this church's religious activities but only with its 'political' activities."

The court held a hearing on the UUA complaint on January 17, 1972, but decided no injunction was required at that time because all grand jury subpoenas had been withdrawn. However, the judge made it clear that if a new subpoena were issued, a court hearing would be held before the bank would be compelled to turn over any UUA records to government agents. Also during the hearing, the U.S. attorney filed a memorandum indicating the strong likelihood that Beacon Press officials would be prosecuted for criminal activity.

The following day, U.S. attorneys asked the court to lift its temporary stay of the investigation, but the judge denied their request. Attorneys for Senator Gravel then succeeded in obtaining a full review by the Supreme Court of the January 7 immunity decision of the Appeals Court: The senator sought to have his senatorial immunity apply to Beacon Press in republishing the papers he had made public in June 1971. UUA attorneys filed amicus curiae briefs in the Supreme Court, which stayed the investigation of the UUA until a decision could be rendered on the issues raised by Senator Gravel.

Later in January, I became concerned that there was too little awareness among the media and general public of what the government was doing to Beacon Press and our denomination, so I embarked on a campaign to spread the word. I wanted to inform as many people as possible about what was occurring and to explain the major issues and principles underlying our actions. I was convinced that, though we hoped to win in the courts, the strongest weapons we had were public awareness and public opinion. I conducted briefing sessions for Unitarian Universalist leaders as well as those of other religious bodies in seven major metropolitan areas: Washington, Chicago, Denver, San Francisco, Los Angeles, Boston, and New York. While in those areas, I also gave interviews to newspapers and broadcast media. In Chicago, for example, Studs Terkel devoted a one-hour radio program to conversing with me about our denomination's experiences relating to the Pentagon Papers and the government's investigation, and two of that city's largest newspapers published editorials of support, as did a number of leading newspapers in other parts of the nation. I also spoke to Unitarian Universalist congregations and district meetings as well as to college students. Gobin Stair arranged for me to address the annual meeting of the Association of American Publishers, and I also spoke at the annual meeting of the American Library Association, both of which issued statements of support.

The UUA board passed a resolution strongly endorsing and supporting the actions I had taken "in resisting the federal government's efforts to subpoena the financial and other records of the Association and of Beacon Press, and in alerting the denomination and the nation to the serious threat to freedom of religion and of association represented by the government's actions. . . . For the first time in the history of our country, the federal government is attempting to subpoena the financial records of a national religious organization, including the names of its members and contributors. . . . The Board of Trustees of the Unitarian Universalist Association is determined to resist this unwarranted and unconstitutional attack. We will fight it in the courts and in the forum of public opinion. . . . Freedom is precious and must ever be defended." The board also created the Legal Fund for Religious Freedom to generate and receive financial support to help defray the mounting legal costs of resisting the government's actions.

We received expressions of support from a large number of individual Unitarian Universalist ministers and congregations, as well as the leadership of district organizations, ministerial schools, and the Unitarian Universalist Ministers Association. Among other religious leaders and groups who conveyed their support were the president of the National Council of Churches, president of the American Ethical Union, bishop of the United Methodist Church of the Boston area, Board of Homeland Missions of the United Church of Christ, executive of the New England synod of the United Presbyterian Church, general secretary and Board of Directors of the Massachusetts Council of Churches, and manager of the committees on publications of the First Church of Christ Scientist in Boston. Additional religious bodies expressing their support included the Union of American Hebrew Congregations, the Central Conference of American Rabbis, and the Friends meeting of Lake Forest, Illinois. The U.S. Catholic Conference offered to "render appropriate legal assistance, if requested, to the counsel for the Beacon Press."

In March 1972, the UUA distributed a special information packet to all Unitarian Universalist congregations. It included suggestions concerning how individual members could help, and an audiotape that contained a brief description of key Pentagon Papers events through February followed by an address I had given at a district meeting. During that speech, I said it was "rather chilling to note that the entire investigation is being conducted by the Internal Security Division," directed from the highest levels of the Justice Department.

The packet also provided brief responses from Gobin Stair and me to the question: Why did we publish *The Senator Gravel Edition of the Pentagon Papers*? Two major reasons I cited were our concerns regarding "peace and war, and the functioning of representative democracy in a highly complex society." Referring to Gravel's statement that hundreds of thousands of needless deaths would have been averted if the true facts had been known by the American people, I said we believed that "in publishing the full version of the Pentagon Papers, we will help reduce the likelihood of our nation becoming involved again in a similar situation." I went on to point out that the "functioning or malfunctioning of our democratic form of government is the subject of the Pentagon Papers and a primary reason for our giving them wider distribution. The issue is whether the American public has the role of central participant in the democratic process, or passive observer of government actions."

Referring to the nature of the religious experience for Unitarians and Universalists, Gobin Stair said, "The dialogue of publishing is for us similar to the dialogue of the pulpit, a part of our active development of principle. . . . A religious press for us is a part of the social process—and as such we declare the necessity in this society to enhance and protect the democratic dialogue: the right to know, the right to publish, and the right to disagree."

Another item included in the March information packet was an "Outline of Issues and Principles Involved in the Government's Investigation of UUA Financial Records and UUA Legal Action Against the Justice Department and FBI and Grand Jury." Alongside the list of issues and principles were brief explanations and examples of their relevance to our situation. Those cited were religious freedom, freedom of association, freedom of the press, senatorial immunity, government intimidation and harassment and repression of legitimate dissent, misuse of the power of the FBI and Justice Department, misuse of grand jury, invasion of privacy, and misuse of secrecy by government.

I wrote in a March 1972 *UU World* article that "the right of religious groups to resist compulsory disclosures of their membership has been established by the Supreme Court. . . . At the core is religious freedom and freedom of association—not only for ourselves but for others." For us, those two issues and the power of intimidation constituted reality, not mere conjecture. I recall being struck by the fact that wherever I spoke to a group about our Pentagon Papers situation, invariably a member of the audience would ask, "If I buy a copy of the Pentagon Papers, am I subject to investigation? Will a file be opened on me?"

A few weeks later, the *UU World* published a letter from a member of a Unitarian Universalist congregation in western Massachusetts, in which he recounted an illustrative incident. He said that on a recent Sunday, at the usual discussion session following the service, he played the Pentagon Papers audiotape we had distributed in the UUA information packet. A young couple had attended the morning service that day for the first time and seemed greatly interested and friendly. They chatted with several members of congregation, drank coffee, arranged to have their names placed on the church's mailing list, and then joined the discussion meeting to listen to the tape. After the discussion session had ended, the two approached the leader and one said, "Please do not put my name on your mailing list. . . . I am very interested in your church, but I have a job with [XYZ] company and I have to have a security check so that I can deal with top-secret papers. I can't afford to have my name associated with you—not after what I heard on that tape. You know how it is, a job, car payments. . . ."

Publishers Weekly printed the entire text of my speech in its May 22 issue. The Seventh Day Adventists published a full-page account of our situation in the May/June issue of their national magazine *Liberty*. The *Saturday Review* featured a discussion of the entire case in the "Up Front" section of its June 10 issue.

The Supreme Court decided the *Gravel* case by a five-to-four majority on June 29, 1972, ruling that the speech or debate clause of the Constitution does not immunize from grand jury inquiry the private publication of documents that a single senator in his official capacity has made public. There was no ruling on the First Amendment claims of the UUA—the freedoms of press, association, and religion—as those issues were not before the court. Justice Rehnquist voted with the majority. Justice Douglas said in dissent, "The story of the Pentagon Papers is a chronicle of suppression of vital decisions to protect the reputations and political hides of men who worked an amazingly successful scheme of deception on the American people." Douglas stated he had no choice but to rule that "here the government, not the press, is lawless."

The effect of the Supreme Court decision was to reopen the Pentagon Papers case. Consequently I issued a statement declaring that the UUA would resist harassment, noting that the "divided court decision means Beacon Press and the UUA are not protected from investigation and prosecution under the speech or debate clause of the Constitution." I affirmed that if the Justice Department chose to resume the investigation through broad grand jury subpoenas, we intended to resist in court to the limit of our ability, primarily on grounds of religious freedom, freedom of association, and freedom of the press.

On July 25, the Supreme Court decision became effective and the stay of the investigation expired. The government again was free to subpoena UUA bank records, but in that event—because of our legal action initiated January 11—there would be a court hearing before the bank would be compelled to turn over any UUA records to government agents. Three days later, U.S. attorneys requested that the federal court in Boston dismiss the UUA complaint of January 11 regarding the FBI investigation, but the court took no action.

Meanwhile, Gobin Stair was subpoenaed to testify as a witness at the criminal trial of Daniel Ellsberg and Anthony Russo in Los Angeles. He was ordered to bring with him the manuscript of the Pentagon Papers and all records reflecting the costs of publishing the Pentagon Papers, the price paid for the document, and all agreements with the source of the Pentagon Papers, including remuneration. At an emergency meeting of the Association of American Publishers in New York, I announced Gobin's receipt of the subpoena to an audience of 170 top executives and editors representing the nation's leading commercial and university publishing houses. The special meeting had been called by the Association's Freedom to Read Committee following the Supreme Court decision in the *Gravel* case. Chairman Robert Bernstein, president of Random House, received an ovation when he called upon the publishers to raise $100 thousand to help the UUA with the expenses of defending First Amendment freedoms. He characterized the Justice Department's harassment of the UUA and the threatened prosecution of Beacon Press officials as "a sad, shabby affair."

In an editorial titled "Freedom Alert" on July 17, 1972, the *New York Times* stated, "The government's harassment of Beacon Press and its concurrent fishing expedition into the wider affairs of the parent religious association imperil not only press freedom but constitutional rights involving religion and association as well. ... All Americans have common cause with the publishers and the church association to be apprehensive over this threat to fundamental freedoms." The *New York Post* printed a similar editorial on July 19 under the title "Thou Shalt Not Print."

Alexander Hoffman, vice president of Doubleday Publishers, wrote an article that appeared in the September 2 issue of the *New York Times* in which, after reviewing the chronology of events associated with the Pentagon Papers, he said,

> What is at stake here transcends party politics and does not involve the difficult judgment concerning the propriety of the original release of the Pentagon Papers. For better or for worse the papers were in the public domain from the outset of Beacon's involvement with the project. They view putting the information in print form as a public service, and they undoubtedly will lose money on it. . . . What the government is doing in this case is using the grand jury process to harass, intimidate, and thereby restrict the broader dissemination of information already in the public domain which the government does not want to have broader circulation.

Hoffman said that one indication the government was succeeding was that there had been "almost complete lack of coverage of this case in other media, particularly broadcast media, although it has been brought to their attention through the Association of American Publishers." He concluded by declaring that the government's "claim that Beacon Press was guilty of criminal activity in acquiring and not returning stolen government documents, even though the entire contents of their books were already part of the public record" was "a line of reasoning that suggests either Lewis Carroll or Joseph Goebbels."

Just as the Ellsberg-Russo trial was beginning in Los Angeles in the fall of 1972, the judge ordered a temporary delay, so we postponed determining our specific response to the Gobin Stair subpoena. The November 1 issue of *UU World* included a fundraising advertisement for contributions to the Mike Gravel Congressional Defense Fund to help with his legal expenses; though the Senate supported the principle of congressional immunity, it refused to share any of Gravel's legal costs. In early November, I addressed the directors of the United Church of

Christ Board for Homeland Ministries, who then voted to endorse and support the UUA in our "response to governmental intrusion." They also voted unanimously with no abstentions to contribute $1 thousand to help defray legal costs incurred in our resistance to "the serious threat to freedom of religion."

On November 28, the government dismissed the grand jury in Boston that had been investigating the Pentagon Papers case, but that did not mean the government's investigation of the UUA and Beacon Press had concluded. In a statement published in the December 1 *UU World*, I said,

> It appears we have been successful in resisting the grand jury's attempts to obtain copies of our denomination's financial records at the bank. However, statements from Justice Department officials demonstrate that there is a continuing threat of government action against the UUA and Beacon Press following the Ellsberg trial. . . . Although we have won another round, we certainly cannot relax.

In May 1973, Group W television stations broadcast an interview with me about our FBI-Pentagon Papers situation, as part of a documentary titled "Freedom and Security: The Uncertain Balance." The program was a study of civil liberties in the United States and the increasing stresses and strains on them from a society in transition. Using illustrations of cases where society was trading off liberty against security, the documentary dealt with federal and local surveillance, aspects of the grand jury system, invasion of privacy, and the role of informers as agents provocateurs.

I noted in my annual report to the 1973 UUA General Assembly that some of the people involved in the infamous Watergate affair (and later convicted as felons) were those who directed the Justice Department's investigation and harassment of the UUA after Beacon Press published the Pentagon Papers:

> Two weeks ago a television executive in New York said to me that our experience—what happened to our denomination —was the "appetizer for Watergate." What has come out of

the Watergate revelations has been exactly what we as a denomination and others have been trying to warn the public in the United States about for more than a year. Three of the persons who have been connected in newspaper stories with the Watergate revelations are those who apparently were directing the government investigation and harassment against us and other dissenting groups. All the time they were accusing us of criminal activities, and threatening to prosecute our staff members, and preaching law and order, they themselves apparently were connected with activities that are destructive of democratic institutions.

Later in the report I affirmed that "we in this denomination have confidence in the democratic process. We want to make known our determination to resist every government intrusion upon constitutional liberties and to encourage others also to resist. We as a religious movement are qualified by our nature, by our heritage, and indeed by our recent experience to play a significant role at this time in our history to help arrest and reverse the ominous trend affecting constitutional liberties."

The Ellsberg-Russo criminal trial resumed after the temporary delay and Gobin Stair prepared to travel to Los Angeles in response to his subpoena. I was advised by UUA special counsel to expect a similar subpoena any day. He said his job was to keep Gobin and me out of jail, and I recall spending a Sunday afternoon with the attorney in the living room of my home preparing for my expected appearance at the Los Angeles trial.

Ellsberg had been indicted on a dozen felony charges for leaking the Pentagon Papers and faced the possibility of a sentence of 115 years in federal prison. Evidence surfaced during the trial, however, that the "White House Plumbers" had violated Ellsberg's constitutional rights by breaking into his psychiatrist's office in 1971 and examining confidential files in an effort to discredit him. They also illegally wiretapped Ellsberg. The Plumbers were an extralegal, covert operations team organized at the highest levels of the executive branch of the federal government—the same group responsible for the notorious 1972 Watergate break-in.

Because of those revelations concerning the government's illegal actions against Ellsberg, as well as other prosecutorial irregularities, the federal judge in Los Angeles declared a mistrial in May 1973. All charges against Ellsberg and Russo were dismissed. The judge said the government's conduct "offended a sense of justice" and "placed the case in such a posture that it precludes the fair, dispassionate resolution of these issues by a jury." The judge also ruled that, because of the government's conduct, the defendants could not be tried a second time. Gobin and I were able to forget about having to appear in federal court in Los Angeles.

The final court proceedings concerning the UUA and the Pentagon Papers occurred in Boston in February 1974. The government stated in federal court that it did not intend to pursue investigating—or seeking or serving a subpoena on—UUA bank records. Consequently, UUA counsel requested that the case be dismissed without prejudice and the court agreed, which meant the court would promptly take the matter up again if the FBI were to resume investigating our bank records.

Contemplating those thirty-one months of our Pentagon Papers experience, I can draw no other conclusion than that the overall intent of the government's actions was to create fear and to have a chilling effect on our denomination, our people, Beacon Press, and other religious bodies, as well as additional groups and individuals and publishers who might be inclined to engage in activity that could constitute dissent from government policy. I'm grateful to the UUA board and attorneys and staff members, to the Unitarian Universalist congregations and individual members, and to the non-Unitarian Universalist book publishers, religious bodies, newspapers, and other organizations for their support and concrete assistance during our Pentagon Papers experience. I'm proud of them as well for their willingness to speak out in a time of fear and intimidation.

Recently I read through multiple documents concerning those

events of more than thirty years ago, feeling at times as though I were living in a parallel universe. I also found myself wondering what would happen to the UUA at the hands of our government if the same decision were made today to publish similar documents. Senator Gravel and the UUA believed that publishing the Pentagon Papers would help reduce the likelihood of the nation embarking again on a similar venture. But at this writing—in view of recent reports of forged documents, fabricated information, and distorted intelligence being used to rally our nation for the Iraq war, plus the government's extreme obsession with secrecy— one has to question whether the lesson has been learned.

It is an eerie feeling to read the words of Senator Gravel, saying that had the true facts been known by the American people "the needless deaths of hundreds of thousands . . . would have been averted," or that "we have created, in the last quarter century, a new culture, protected from the influences of American life by the shield of secrecy." Or those of Beacon Press editor-in-chief Arnold Tovell about "exactly how a well-meaning nation could have committed such a colossal blunder in its foreign affairs." Or Beacon Press director Gobin Stair writing that "we declare the necessity in this society to enhance and protect the democratic dialogue: the right to know, the right to publish, and the right to disagree." Or my words to the 1973 General Assembly delegates:

> What bothers me most about the continuing tragedy of the Watergate situation is that some government leaders still do not realize that individual liberty is at the heart of the kind of society and kind of government that we mean to have and which they profess to uphold. They fail to realize that what threatens one threatens all. They fail to realize that the problems of society today cannot be solved by repressing freedom, that freedom of expression must be protected, that the public's right and duty to know must be safeguarded, that government must encourage freedom of expression, not suppress it.

Not long ago a friend expressed a view different from mine. He said the unveiling of secret government manipulation in the Pentagon Papers forever demolished the illusion that government can be trusted more than other human ventures. He suggested that the current ability of the media to raise fundamental challenges to the government is rooted in the lessons of the Pentagon Papers, and that every time the government betrays the public trust the media will be quicker to call the government to account.

I would like to think him right, but the recent performance of the U.S. press—in failing to probe behind the government's distorted information and propagandistic news handouts that led to the Iraq war and continue still—gives me little cause in the near term for such hope. Perhaps a renewed awareness of the atrocious governmental deceptiveness and destructiveness related to the Iraq war can fulfill that hope.

Identity and "Sharing In Growth" Programs

WHEN I BEGAN my campaign for UUA president during the fall of 1968, I stated that our movement was in severe crisis affecting programs, finances, attitudes, and identity. In my annual report to the 1970 General Assembly, I named Unitarian Universalist identity as foremost among my priorities for the ensuing year. Consequently, in March 1971 we launched a fifteen-month exploration of Unitarian Universalist identity. The goal of the program was to achieve throughout our denomination a clearer awareness and articulation of answers to the questions: What is a Unitarian Universalist today? What is Unitarian Universalist religion today?

The core of the enterprise comprised twenty-three elements: specific actions and activities in which we could arrive at a more clearly articulated expression of our religious identity. Coordinated by the UUA Department of Communications, the program involved congregations, ministers, individual Unitarian Universalists, districts, ministerial schools, twenty organizations, and the General Assembly. Throughout those fifteen months, the entire professional staff gave priority to Unitarian Universalist identity as a major concern of the UUA. During the course of the program, I found the lengthy guest editorials and readers' statements in the *UU World* especially helpful to me personally. I also was impressed by the multiple and varied activities undertaken by numerous congregations.

In an article initiating the program, I wrote,

> Many persons have expressed a need for a more clearly articulated contemporary expression of our religious identity. They seek a clearer enunciation not so much of what we may have been in the 1830s or 1950s but what are we today in the 1970s.
>
> The program . . . is a process. No fixed and final answers are expected. It will be of aid in putting our aspirations and activities in clearer perspective. The problem of Unitarian Universalist identity is a basic one for our movement at the present time, pervading almost all facets of our life as congregations and as a denomination. The problem of identity becomes manifest in numerous areas—for example, the role expectations of ministers and expectations of congregations concerning their ministers; religious education; the beliefs and motivation of members; extension; worship; social action; advertising; publications; programming by congregations; ministerial education; and many others.

I pointed out that in devising the program we had deliberately avoided creating a committee or commission to attempt to articulate Unitarian Universalist identity. A few months later, I posed the question: "What do we have in our religion today in addition to freedom?" I said the Identity program "simply is a process for sharing by groups and individuals in an effort to help one another and our movement as a whole in attaining a clearer awareness and articulation of what Unitarian Universalist religion is today. Such an articulation is necessary if we are to be more effective. It has to do not with what we have been but what we are becoming."

When the Identity program was introduced in 1971, I stated that it would be of value to our free religious cause and enable us to be a more effective religious community. In retrospect, I believe the statement was accurate. The program was a type that might not attract a great deal of attention today, yet it was critical for our denomination then and laid the foundation for subsequent progress in a number of key respects. It did help individuals and congregations with aspects of their religious life mentioned in the article quoted above. On a larger scale, it infused our movement with significantly strengthened motivation and cohesiveness that were major factors in the support we received during the Pentagon Papers episode; the success of our Sharing In Growth program; the markedly different nature of the 1972 and 1973 General Assemblies; and our eventual turnaround in vitality, optimism, and personal religious searching, as well as attaining our annual financial goals.

Membership Numbers

In 1969 and 1970, we took actions to assure that our denomination's published membership numbers reflected reality insofar as possible. The 1975 General Assembly approved a UUA bylaws change that formalized a major aspect of that endeavor. The change declared that to be considered active a congregation must conduct regular religious services; hold at least one business meeting annually, elect its own officers, and maintain adequate records of membership; and make a financial contribution to the Association.

In my last five years as president, the number of our active congregations fell from 1,019 to 1,000, while our adult membership declined at an average annual rate of 1.3 percent. Though our membership did decrease somewhat, we pretty much held our own compared to larger religious bodies; mainline Protestant denominations experienced a general decline in membership throughout my tenure.

Events and trends in the general culture also had their effect. For example, with the exception of fundamentalists and Pentecostals, other denominations in that period experienced reduced giving to continental operations, huge cuts in staff, and declines in membership; and the two recessions after 1969 caused difficulty not only for the nation but for our denomination as well.

Sharing In Growth

During my 1972 annual report to the General Assembly, I outlined a proposed program for growth, one that was designed to do more than just add new members. In presenting the program, I cited the original meanings of the terms evangelism and spirit: evangelism as bringing good news and spirit as the animating force within human beings. I said,

> We are distinguished from traditional religion and also from contemporary secular society by our spirit. That spirit is less to be defined than experienced, but once felt I would even dare call it a "holy spirit" that enables us to grow, broadens our outlook, deepens our insight, and warms our lives. It is up to us now to articulate that spirit and make it known to others.

The UUA board approved the Sharing In Growth program "for extending and strengthening Unitarian Universalist religion" in October of that year. It constituted the first major change in the direction of efforts toward denominational growth since the 1940s. The new approach was primarily aimed at secular society, not at people in organized religions who had been unable to find answers to their spiritual needs. In presenting the proposal to the board, I stated, "If our denomination is to grow—if we are to extend and strengthen Unitarian Universalist religion, enlarge the influence of our religious outlook, share it with others—our programs and efforts must include the core elements of warmth, depth, breadth, and growth." Other aspects of the program were a clearer articulation of what Unitarian Universalism is today, a description of the difference between secular society and Unitarian Universalist religion, and celebration reflecting and expressing the four core elements. The undertaking—featuring volunteers and focusing on locales with the greatest potential—involved "experimentation, research, evaluation, and new efforts in publicity and promotion, including television, to encourage the broadest possible understanding of what we are and what we do."

I observed that the four key terms could be equated with more traditional ones:

WARMTH (community): Our attitudes and programs must reflect warmth. Genuine community must be an aspect of our congregations, not just for ourselves but for all who enter our doors. We should reach out to meet different needs that arise from loneliness in people.

DEPTH (ultimate questions): Congregational and denominational programs must put major emphasis on helping persons with personal religion, with exploring ultimate questions. In each congregation, people should come to grips with deep questions of life and death. Though we have no authoritative answers, we can aid in continued search, contemplation, and application.

BREADTH (programs): Local church programs should have variety and balance to meet a diversity of personal needs and interests. There should be opportunities for community action, social gatherings, and education, as well as worship, aesthetics, and small group programs.

GROWTH (sharing): Growth is another word for sharing—openly sharing our Unitarian Universalist religion. Although historically we have had few missionaries and have criticized traditional endeavors to convert people and save souls, the plain fact is that our own strength today is the direct result of past deliberate efforts to extend our faith and grow in size.

In visits to congregations and district meetings, both as UUA president and earlier as a parish minister, I was continually surprised by the large number of Unitarian Universalists who strongly believed we should not try to increase our membership. I never quite understood that attitude, though I assumed it was caused either by an intensely negative experience involving some religious group that exerted enormous pressure on individuals to believe its One True Way or by a highly developed personal sense of privacy. In presenting the Sharing In Growth proposal to the UUA board and denomination, I emphasized that "one of the elements required will be openness, genuine openness among our members to new people."

The practical implementation of the program involved four major aspects:

Teams. At the center of Sharing In Growth were five-member teams of volunteers with leadership experience in congregations, "committed persons who deeply care about the continued strength of our Unitarian Universalist religion, persons whose warmth, understanding, and enthusiasm can be contagious." Each team was assembled from a specified congregation or area and, after specialized training, made periodic visits to a designated congregation. The composition of each team reflected as much diversity of interest, experience, talent, and age as possible.

Focused effort. The program's major efforts were focused on situations that seemed to offer the greatest potential for growth, leadership development, creating programs others could use, and increasing cooperation and sharing among existing congregations.

Research-Experimentation-Evaluation. Among the questions to be answered were: Why do certain congregations grow despite a general pattern of church memberships leveling off? Why do many persons attuned to Unitarian Universalist religion not join our congregations? What are the measurable results in those congregations with which Sharing In Growth teams work?

Publicity and Promotion. Because a key factor in growth can be public awareness of who we are and what we are doing, techniques and materials for use with newspapers, radio, and television were part of the program.

During the four months following its initiation, thirty-eight congregations expressed interest in participating in the Sharing In Growth program, and the New England Interdistrict Council provided funds for a pilot project involving six New Hampshire and Vermont churches. In March 1973, the UUA board accepted a two-year grant from the Unitarian Universalist congregation in Plandome, New York, to provide funds for the Sharing In Growth program (see the chapter "The Veatch Program and Holdeen Trusts"). The special grant enabled the UUA to develop materials to aid in the extension of liberal religion and to hire two full-time staff members: a director for volunteer teams, who worked with congregations and recruited, trained, and advised Sharing In Growth teams, and a director for evaluation and research, who designed and conducted research and evaluation projects.

Later in 1973, the UUA arranged a conference on using the media to promote Unitarian Universalist growth, featuring presenters with extensive experience in educational and cable television. The participants viewed television tapes produced by a group in Toronto that had completed more than sixty half-hour television programs sponsored by the Canadian Unitarian Council. They also viewed a program from a CBS television series "Make Up Your Mind," which was based on the UUA *Decision Making* curriculum and produced in Philadelphia. In subsequent months, a group of Unitarian Universalist volunteers, residents of the New York metropolitan area who were associated with advertising, created and tested a series of newspaper and magazine advertisements.

As we proceeded into 1974, twenty congregations of varying sizes were enrolled in the Sharing In Growth program in such disparate locales as Nebraska, New York, Missouri, California, Alabama, and Illinois. The number of congregations accepted into the program was necessarily limited because of the cost and UUA staff time required, but all our congregations had access to resource materials developed during the three-year span of Sharing In Growth. The research-and-evaluation aspect of the program included a questionnaire that as of April 1974 had been answered by four thousand members of Unitarian Universalist congregations as well as two thousand nonmembers; its findings were applicable throughout our denomination.

In early 1974, the Plandome congregation changed its method of contributing to the Association. Instead of approving individual grants for discrete projects from its Veatch funds as in the past, the congregation voted to contribute large annual block amounts for a two-year period. The resolution specified no limitations on the annual block grants except that the UUA allocate $98 thousand to continue the Sharing In Growth program.

Sharing In Growth was designed to be a three-year program with three phases, the first focusing on certain selected congregations. The second was based in large part on knowledge gained from working with churches and fellowships during the previous phase and was developed with the assistance of laity and ministers who were involved in that first stage. The major purpose of the second phase was to make the program more widely available; the UUA offered Sharing In Growth to any congregation seeking to develop a stronger sense of community, improve its programming, intensify the quality of its religious commitment, and develop its decision-making process and membership.

The Sharing In Growth program sponsored a *UU World* insert in September of 1975 that contained four instruments as examples of the types of actions any congregation could take—in board or committee meetings, in Sunday services, in discussion or study groups, and among individual members—to achieve the program's goals. The insert also included detailed data about Unitarian Universalists from questionnaires that had been completed by twenty-eight congregations.

That issue of *UU World* described Sharing In Growth as "a program for Unitarian Universalist congregations across the continent, a program that is a process for enhancing the quality of life within each of our societies . . . for continuous renewal and growth toward greater *warmth* of relationships, *breadth* of programming, and *depth* of spirit. The process involves congregations in gathering information about themselves, setting goals and agreeing on

priorities for their own future development, and working with selected teams of laypeople toward the achievement of their hopes
and dreams." The newspaper insert emphasized that any congregation could send for a Sharing In Growth packet, self-study material, a description of the goal-setting process, or publicity and
promotion assistance. Churches and fellowships could also apply
to participate in a full Sharing In Growth program, which included the team process.

The third and more permanent phase of Sharing In Growth
entailed incorporating its results into our denomination's ongoing
life. In June 1976, the UUA board received the final report of the
program, and in October *UU World* published an article based on
a report and evaluation prepared by Sharing In Growth staff
members. The report indicated that the program had directly involved forty-eight congregations and approximately five hundred
individual laypersons who had served as team members. At least
one-quarter of all Unitarian Universalist congregations across the
continent were touched by the program. The evaluation results
were largely positive with respect to participating congregations
having accomplished their goals. Statistically there was growth of
membership and budget in all the pilot situations studied.

As I left office in the spring of 1977, Sharing In Growth commissions, committees, task forces, and teams were active in numerous districts and clusters, working to strengthen Unitarian
Universalist religion. Clearly, Sharing In Growth—and the
Identity program that served as the groundwork for it—had a significant impact on our denomination.

The Veatch Program
and Holdeen Trusts

WHILE WE WERE contending with the immediate difficulties of my early months in office, I took two additional steps to improve the long-term organizational and financial health of the UUA. One concerned the Veatch program of the Unitarian Universalist congregation in Plandome, New York, and the other involved the Jonathan Holdeen trusts. The Veatch program was incalculably valuable in helping our Association survive as an effective continental denomination, and along with the Holdeen trusts, it has provided tens of millions of dollars to the UUA throughout the past three decades.

In 1943, a small number of religious liberals in Port Washington, New York, founded a Unitarian fellowship that subsequently became a church situated in Plandome and since 1993 has been the Unitarian Universalist Congregation at Shelter Rock. Carolyn Veatch became a member of the congregation during its early years when the group met in a large house. Her husband, Arthur Veatch, was a world-renowned geologist who died in the late 1930s, leaving her royalty interests in German oil fields, which produced no royalties prior to the 1940s. Because her claim lacked backing due to World War II devastation, Mrs. Veatch sought help in 1948 from the minister and a lawyer member of the congregation. The success of the ensuing investigation allowed Mrs. Veatch to begin receiving royalties, which she shared with the church in her lifetime and bequeathed to the congregation when she died in 1953. Though the annual royalty payments were relatively small in the 1950s, they increased substantially after the fields produced natural gas; the church began receiving millions of dollars every year. The congregation wisely separated the Veatch monies from its normal operating funds by creating the Veatch program, now known as the Unitarian Universalist Veatch Program at Shelter Rock. Its purpose was—and remains—to make grants in support of Unitarian Universalist organizations that foster the growth and development of our denomination and that increase Unitarian Universalist involvement in social action. The program also supports other organizations whose goals reflect the principles of Unitarian Universalist religion. During the years I was UUA president, a committee elected by the congregation administered the Veatch program, though any grant the committee approved above a certain amount required a vote by the congregation for final approval.

When I became president in 1969, the Plandome congregation had no confidence in the UUA administration because of the preceding administration's financial and spending practices. I spent an enormous amount of time meeting with members of the congregation and the Veatch Committee, explaining my approach to the UUA's problems and trying to regain their confidence in the UUA as a trustworthy, accountable recipient of their grants. I was finally successful; the Plandome congregation and Veatch committee approved new grants to the UUA. Throughout my two terms, I continued to meet with the Veatch Committee and members of the congregation to answer questions, and explain how their grants were being spent. A representative of the committee attended all UUA board meetings as an invited observer.

In 1970, the Veatch program funded a full-time staff position at UUA headquarters to encourage and assist with bequests to the Association. During the same year, the Plandome congregation and Community Church of New York were leaders among the churches that lent money to the UUA so we could immediately liquidate our long-term bank loans. In the fall of 1971, the Plandome church offered to lend $100 thousand to Beacon Press for working capital in connection with publishing the Pentagon Papers (see the chapter "Pentagon Papers"). In 1972, the congregation gave $250 thousand to the UUA for a special fund to promote racial justice and combat racism, and made additional grants in succeeding years for the same purpose (see the chapter "Black UU Caucus and Black Affairs Council"). In 1973, the UUA accepted a two-year grant from the Veatch program to fund the Sharing In Growth program for extending and strengthening Unitarian Universalist religion (see the chapter "Identity and 'Sharing In Growth' Programs").

The Plandome church changed the nature of its Veatch allocations to annual block grants in 1974, replacing the practice of funding individual UUA projects. The congregation voted to give $600 thousand to the Association—twice the sum it had contributed the previous year—to create a grants section of the annual UUA budget for the purpose of funding special programs and services that we would otherwise be unable to undertake. The grant specified no additional limitations on the annual amount, except that $98 thousand be allocated for continuing the Sharing In Growth program. In discussing the Plandome gift with the UUA board, I emphasized that the grant funds would be available to support some special undertakings, but basic UUA programs and services would continue to depend on the contributions of congregations and individuals to our annual program fund.

Besides the bequests program, racial justice fund, and Sharing In Growth program, some of the projects and programs supported by the new grants section were religious education curriculum units, programs on aging, education for professional religious leadership, district programs, UUA and Beacon Press fundraising, publicity, youth programs, career counseling for older ministers, and the Washington Office for Social Concern.

Thirty-five percent of all Veatch grants between 1969 and 1974 were for denominational purposes; the UUA received two-thirds of those gifts and the remainder went to organizations such as the Unitarian Universalist Service Committee, International Association for Religious Freedom, Unitarian Universalist United Nations office, Church of the Larger Fellowship, and Unitarian Universalist ministerial schools and summer camps, among others. The Plandome church continued to support a highly successful building-loan program to facilitate the continued growth of member congregations by providing affordable financing to acquire ownership of a building or to expand or renovate existing facilities.

The UUA trustees adopted the practice of prioritizing programs and projects that were proposed for grant funding. In January 1975, the top nine priorities were the religious education curriculum, fundraising, the Sharing In Growth program, education for professional religious leadership, the bequests program, publicity, the Office of Gay Concerns, the Beacon Press reserve fund, and district programs. The board prioritized sixteen additional programs to receive financial support if funds became available.

During a December 1975 meeting with the Veatch Committee, I proposed that, beginning with the 1977–1978 fiscal year, the amount of the Plandome congregation's annual block grants to the UUA would equal the total amount all other congregations had contributed to the UUA annual program fund in the prior fiscal year. The intended effect of this proposal was to provide an incentive for congregations to contribute to the annual program fund, beginning with their first dollar. At its January 1976 meeting, the UUA Board voted to support the proposal. Six weeks later, the Plandome congregation voted to change the basis on which it made annual contributions to the UUA: For each of the two fiscal years beginning July 1, 1977, the congregation would contribute a total amount equal to the amount other congregations had given to the UUA annual program fund during the previous year. In a letter to the president of the Plandome congregation expressing our appreciation, after noting that the incentive aspect of the new approach would enable the UUA to provide better services and programs, I commended the congregation "for its willingness to share, and to be of practical help to the other congregations in our common free religious cause."

Concurrent with those developments were discussions with Veatch representatives aimed at establishing permanent funds, with the resulting income used to support UUA programs. After I left office, such funds did come into existence, resulting in tens of millions of dollars being made available to the UUA. Two examples were a $20-million endowment announced in 1979, which was soon followed by a $15-million permanent fund for ministerial education.

It wasn't just monetary contributions that made the Veatch program so unique and special. It was the spirit of sharing, a sense of "we are all in this together," of genuine gratitude for all the denomination and other congregations—past and present—had done to contribute to the Plandome congregation's existence and growth. It was the way the Plandome church disbursed its Veatch funds: its careful consideration of proposed programs and potential recipients, its sound and balanced approach to fulfilling the charitable and fiduciary responsibilities the congregation voluntarily assumed.

It would be difficult to exaggerate the contribution of the Plandome church in enabling our Association to continue as an effective liberal religious continental denomination. In an era of deep and divisive crises, the congregation, through its Veatch program, acted quietly and responsibly to maintain valuable programs and underwrite new approaches to cope with the problems besetting our religious movement. The congregation's contribution to our denomination is of inestimable worth and benefit, for which we and our descendants should remain deeply appreciative.

Holdeen

My involvement with the Holdeen trusts began in the fall of 1969, when I asked the UUA treasurer about a particular check I had received in the mail. He suggested I discuss it with UUA counsel, who told me about Jonathan Holdeen and the multiple trusts he established during his lifetime.

Born in 1881, Jonathan Holdeen was an eccentric lawyer and businessman in New York City. After living in the metropolitan area for a number of years, he moved north to a small town in Dutchess County where he lived until his death in 1967. Holdeen was interested in Benjamin Franklin's bequests of two-hundred-year trusts for the cities of Boston and Philadelphia. He also was intrigued with the theory that taxes could be abolished if a person were to leave money to the government in trust for a period of five hundred or one thousand years, because the initial sum would increase to trillions or quadrillions of dollars.

Beginning in 1945, Jonathan Holdeen placed millions of dollars in various trusts that lasted five hundred or one thousand years and named the state of Pennsylvania as ultimate beneficiary. He chose Pennsylvania because Franklin had lived there, and Holdeen believed its courts would therefore be amenable to upholding the legality of the trusts. The UUA had an interest in several of the trusts, namely, those in which Holdeen named the American Unitarian Association and its successors, which included the UUA, as the recipient of annual income. But a special formula limited the income distributed to our Association each year: The UUA received only one-thousandth of the annual income in year one, two-thousandths of the annual income in year two, three-thousandths of the annual income in year three, and so on. All the remaining annual income accumulated and remained in the total endowment of each trust.

When I first met with counsel, I learned that two of Jonathan Holdeen's relatives and his lawyer were the trustees for the UUA trusts and for dozens of other Holdeen trusts. I also learned that the Internal Revenue Service was challenging the trusts as an elaborate scheme by Holdeen to avoid taxes and benefit his family. I was already aware that my predecessor as UUA president had visited the lead trustee every year to collect annual checks for relatively small sums. I believed the UUA wasn't receiving the income to which it was entitled. Counsel agreed and also expressed the view that the long-term cumulative scheme of the trusts was probably illegal.

I decided the UUA should request an accounting from the trustees and, if we didn't receive a satisfactory accounting, we should sue the trustees to obtain the amount of money to which the UUA was legally entitled. As I was arriving at this decision, counsel told me I would never get to oversee use of any of the funds our Association might obtain; even if our litigation were successful, it could be as long as twelve years before any additional money from the trusts would be available for use by the UUA. He proved to be right.

We didn't receive a satisfactory accounting, and consequently the UUA sued the Holdeen trustees in Philadelphia Orphans Court, which had jurisdiction for trusts and estates. UUA lawyers argued that for a charitable trust to accumulate such staggeringly massive amounts of money for five hundred or one thousand years was unreasonable, contrary to public policy, and therefore void.

Meanwhile the IRS challenge to the trusts was proceeding through U.S. Tax Court. The government's position was that the trusts were a tax-evasion scheme. In addition, the government alleged that the trustees were making loans from UUA trusts to family trusts, commingling UUA trust funds with family trust funds, and making joint real estate investments. IRS attorneys also asserted that the books and records of trusts were improvised and incomplete. In 1975, the Tax Court issued its decision against the IRS, finding the UUA trusts to be "valid and genuine."

I was involved with the Holdeen legal proceedings from time to time throughout my two terms in office, giving depositions, meeting with our attorneys to make decisions, consulting with the UUA Board in executive sessions, and traveling to Philadelphia to testify. A few weeks before I left office, the judge in the Philadelphia Orphans Court wrote, "The express purpose [of the five-hundred- and one-thousand-year accumulations] is so visionary, unreasonable, and socially and economically unsound that we must conclude the entire plan is charitably purposeless, contrary to public policy, and hence void." The court nullified the long-term accumulation of income but left the trusts intact in other respects. The ruling granted our Association past and future income from the relevant Holdeen trusts.

The Holdeen trustees appealed the decision, but two years later the Pennsylvania Supreme Court upheld the 1977 ruling of the Philadelphia Orphans Court. That meant the UUA could begin receiving past and future income, which has since amounted to tens of millions of dollars. By 1994, our Association had received $22 million and the amount the UUA was obtaining from the trusts every year was approximately $1 million.

However, litigation involving our Association and the Holdeen trustees did not come to a close when the Pennsylvania Supreme Court affirmed the 1977 decision. Several years after I left office, the UUA brought new multimillion-dollar legal actions against the trustees. The Association alleged mismanagement, self-dealing, gross negligence, and fraud associated with real estate transactions that mixed UUA trusts with private family trusts in a manner that favored family members to the detriment of the UUA. Among specific assertions of Association lawyers were that some properties in UUA trusts had been written off as worthless or had disappeared from trust records with no explanation, that improper loans had been made, and that the assets of UUA and family trusts had been commingled.

Much of the income the UUA has received from Holdeen trusts over the years was designated by Jonathan Holdeen to benefit Asian Indians. Today the Unitarian Universalist Holdeen India Program uses its income to work with disadvantaged people in India, promoting long-term changes that alleviate unjust conditions. The program has supported more than five dozen indigenous organizations throughout several Indian states.

In addition to the Asian Indian bequests, the provisions of two trusts permit the Association to designate other beneficiaries, and through the years the UUA has distributed many millions of dollars derived from those trusts. Recipients have included the International Association for Religious Freedom, International Council of Unitarians and Universalists, World Conference on

Religion and Peace, Partner Church Council, and Liberal Religious Charitable Society.

People frequently ask me if Jonathan Holdeen was a Unitarian. I'm aware of no evidence that he ever entered a Unitarian or Universalist church.

Civil Rights and Liberties

DURING THE YEARS I was president, numerous individual Unitarian Universalists, as well as our congregations and organizations, applied their religious values to social concerns by actively engaging major issues that were roiling in society, including the Vietnam War, abortion, the death penalty, impeachment, and civil rights and liberties.

In February 1972, Americans United for Separation of Church and State sponsored its twenty-fourth national conference. The Washington gathering featured several national and international speakers, and I was invited to address the opening session. My remarks stressed the egregiousness of the current investigation and harassment of our denomination by the Internal Security Division of the Justice Department (see the chapter "Pentagon Papers"), and the never-ending need to vigilantly maintain separation of church and state.

Later that month, in an amicus brief filed in the U.S. Supreme Court case *Tatum v. Laird*, the UUA attacked military surveillance as a violation of First Amendment rights. Several Unitarian Universalist congregations were known to have been the objects of military surveillance, including those in Monterey, California; Evanston, Illinois; and San Antonio, Texas. The National Council of Churches of Christ, American Friends Service Committee, and

Council for Christian Action of the United Church of Christ joined our Association in filing the brief. With U.S. Senator Sam Ervin as our attorney, the UUA brief argued that the rights of groups associated with peace efforts had been infringed on "by an unauthorized, unnecessary, and indiscriminate military program of investigation into their political views, activities, association, and personal lives." I stated that we were "filing this amicus brief because congregations within our own religious denomination have been subject to unwarranted governmental intrusions upon their rights of privacy, freedom of association, and freedom of religion through secret military surveillance of their activities and members."

In the summer of 1972, the American Publishers Association invited the UUA to send a witness to testify in Washington before Senator William Proxmire's committee in support of a bill, the Citizens Privacy Protection Act, to prevent the names of church contributors from unconstitutionally ending up in FBI dossiers. The context of the hearing was that, just before the provisions of a new bank secrecy act were to take effect, legal actions instituted by the American Civil Liberties Union, our Association, and others had halted their implementation. Christopher Raible, the member of our executive staff who represented the UUA, testified that "the FBI did inspect our bank records without our receiving prior notification of the investigation and therefore without our knowledge. . . . The Internal Security Division of the Justice Department and the FBI had in the period from October 20 through November 3 the opportunity to collect without our knowledge the names of donors and members of our Association."

That October, the UUA board approved my recommendation that the UUA join more than twenty national organizations in signing a statement opposing a federal tax credit that would assist in supporting sectarian schools. In early November, I wrote to the chairman of the advisory committee to the U.S. Department of Health, Education, and Welfare about the use of social security numbers, stressing the issue of personal privacy and opposing government abuse of privacy in data-gathering systems. I specifically opposed recommendations of the Social Security Number Task Force, saying that the UUA believes the rights of the individual come first and the computer second. I said that the general posture of using the number for purposes other than the Social Security program should be opposed unless all rights of privacy and due process are protected, and I noted that the "use of the number in data collection and exchange presents currently an unknown level of danger to society."

Early in December 1972, I began meeting with leaders from religious organizations, publishers, and civil liberties groups who were concerned about the ominous trend of what was happening to basic constitutional liberties at the hands of the government. The result was the Conference on American Freedom, conceived and developed primarily during my consultations with Robert Bernstein, president of Random House publishers, and Dean Kelley, director for religious and civil liberties of the National Council of Churches.

The Conference on American Freedom took place in Washington on April 10–11, 1973. Its express purpose was "to make known our determination to resist all government intrusions on constitutional liberties." The eighteen conveners of the conference were top leaders of academic institutions; religious denominations; newspaper, book, and magazine publishing; and national nonprofit organizations. Attending the conference were more than fifty leaders in those fields as well as in civil rights, labor, librarian, and civic groups.

The participants discussed government interference with rights of speech, press, privacy, religion, and association. Six papers on the focal topics were written specifically for the conference and distributed in advance to participants; the authors included Henry Steele Commager, professor of history at Amherst College, and Thomas Emerson, professor of law at Yale University. Senator Sam Ervin—who at that time was chairman of the special committee conducting the Watergate hearings—delivered the keynote speech and Congressman Charles Whalen gave the closing address. Five people who had direct experience with government intrusions on their rights, including nationally known journalists Sander Vanocur and David Halberstam, made oral presentations and participated in the discussions. UUA headquarters personnel served as conference staff, and I presided at the sessions.

A "Statement of Concern" was prepared during the conference and signed by most participants. It said in part,

> Newspaper reporters are jailed, others forced to disclose sources. High government officials threaten television, radio, and newspapers. Government secrecy is expanding. Grand juries are used to harass and intimidate, and repress dissent.
>
> The government is reducing its support and increasing its control of public broadcasting. Government agents routinely obtain copies of personal checks and other records from banks without informing customers. Government agencies engage in political surveillance unrelated to the investigation of any specific crime.
>
> Playing on fears of citizens, the government uses "national security" and "criminal activity" as excuses to suspend the Constitution and violate historic guarantees of freedom.
>
> America's problems cannot be solved by repressing freedom.
>
> The Constitution alone does not guarantee freedom; it cannot protect the independence of citizens unless citizens themselves guard their rights and never lose the will to resist government encroachment. What threatens one, threatens all.

Our Association published papers from the conference in a sixty-three-page book titled *Freedom Papers*. Besides five of the papers written in advance of the conference, the book included the "Statement of Concern," Sander Vanocur's remarks, and the concluding address by Congressman Charles Whalen. The UUA sent copies to numerous libraries and educational institutions and made them available for general purchase.

Illegal operations within the Internal Revenue Service that involved the UUA came to light in November 1974. Consequently I issued the following statement as a press release, and included it as part of a letter I wrote to a number of U.S. senators and congressmen.

What assurance do we have that it will not happen again?

That is the question I would ask senators and congressmen regarding disclosure on November 18 that a secret political intelligence unit operated from within the IRS at the instigation of the White House from 1969 to 1973.

Our denomination was listed among ninety-nine groups investigated. The purpose of the special IRS unit was to gather intelligence data on ideological, militant, subversive, radical, or other organizations. Specific instructions included gathering information on the motives, activities, and attitudes of each organization, as well as sources of funds and names and addresses of contributors and its impact on the general public.

Those IRS operations clearly are unconstitutional. They infringe upon freedoms of religion, speech, and association. Such an IRS unit represents the abuse of government power and the misuse of a government agency for political purposes.

We expect our government to protect our freedoms, not to engage in secret machinations to infringe upon them.

Our denomination is over four hundred years old. Many of our congregations were in existence at the time our nation was founded. We are not a militant, subversive, or radical organization.

There is ample evidence that the government used the IRS, as it used the Justice Department, for repression and harassment of those who dissented from government policy. The IRS disclosures are another example of the inability of the White House to distinguish subversion from honest dissent based on religious and ethical convictions.

We protest. But of what avail is it to protest after the fact? The special IRS unit was disbanded only after its existence was revealed by the Watergate hearings. What guarantee do we have that such an illegal operation will not be conducted again?

Our Association headquarters was located in Boston, the site of one of the most significant struggles for racial desegregation of that period. In early 1975, the UUA joined the newly formed Massachusetts Coalition for Human Rights, composed of more than thirty-eight organizations concerned with attaining high-quality integrated education and nonsegregated open communities throughout the state. In April, the NAACP and the National Student Coalition Against Racism asked thousands of people from around the country to converge on Boston to support school desegregation. I joined with a number of other Unitarian Universalist lay and ministerial leaders in sponsoring the resulting May 17 NAACP National Freedom March on Boston.

The UUA endorsed the march and I wrote a letter to all ministers and leaders of our congregations in the United States encouraging Unitarian Universalists to participate, noting that our Association "through several General Assemblies affirmed support of integrated quality education. The May 17 Boston March is an opportunity to express our support with specific action at a needed time." Unitarian Universalists traveled from around the continent to participate in the march and the subsequent rally on Boston Common. They came from Massachusetts, New York, Virginia, New Jersey, Washington, California, Maryland, and Ontario. Three of us carried the same UUA banner that had been borne in Selma, Alabama, ten years earlier.

In the fall of 1975, Congress was attempting to eliminate the power of the Department of Health, Education, and Welfare to order busing as a remedy for segregated schools, as granted under the 1964 Civil Rights Act. I joined six other religious leaders in sending a telegram to members of the Massachusetts congressional delegation, opposing efforts to undercut school-busing laws. The UUA also joined with the Massachusetts Coalition for Human Rights in calling on the Civil Rights Division of the Justice Department for increased federal protection of students in Boston's public schools, particularly South Boston High School.

The spring of 1976 found Boston a city wracked by violence

stemming from some residents who opposed court-ordered busing to achieve school desegregation. A bomb explosion on April 22 in a courthouse two blocks from UUA headquarters sent a score of people to hospitals. The following morning at the start of the April 23–25 UUA trustees meeting, I suggested the board interrupt its first session so members could march in the "Procession Against Violence" that had been called by the mayor and endorsed by the governor, the NAACP, and other groups. I noted that participation by our Association would be a "visible statement against violence in this city where we have had our headquarters for 150 years." Nearly all board members joined the march.

Later in the spring, I joined a group of Massachusetts religious leaders in a plea to state and federal officials for funds to create summer jobs for Boston youth. That was an especially critical time because of problems originating from the negative reactions to court-ordered busing. Key elements we cited were the thousands of Boston youths who would be unemployed and restless when school was out for the summer and the hardships caused by citywide curfews.

In my annual report to the 1973 General Assembly, I noted,

Although our denomination over the years has had an abiding concern for individual liberty and the functioning of democracy, our own recent UUA experience has served to intensify and deepen that concern. . . . Our Unitarian Universalist movement is qualified by its nature, heritage, and recent experience to play a significant role at this time in history to help arrest and reverse the trend affecting constitutional liberties. We can and we will.

International Activities

As UUA PRESIDENT, my primary focus regarding international religious matters was the International Association for Religious Freedom (IARF), especially its Unitarian member churches in Transylvania, Romania, Hungary, Czechoslovakia, and the United Kingdom, as well as the Free Religious congregations in Germany. Those priorities were grounded in our indebtedness to the Unitarian churches in Transylvania and Britain as the progenitors of our denomination in America; the oppression of the central-European congregations, with their resulting need for help; and the reaching out to American Unitarians by the Free Religious congregations in Germany before and after World War II.

In 1969, the above congregations and denominations were all members of the IARF, along with religious groups in additional European nations, India, and Japan. Especially for Unitarians in central Europe, the IARF was the major instrument for communication and personal contacts among liberal churches and denominations in different nations. Founded in 1900 by the American Unitarian Association as the International Council of Unitarian and Other Religious Thinkers and Workers, the name was changed in 1930 to International Association for Liberal Christianity and Religious Freedom. In 1969, the group's triennial congress met in Boston concurrent with our annual UUA General

Assembly and, on the initiative of UUA delegates, changed the name to International Association for Religious Freedom.

At that time, there was a secretariat composed of three individuals residing in Switzerland, the Netherlands, and the United States, but no one person was responsible for day-to-day IARF operations. A council, consisting of representatives from at least eight countries, exercised general oversight of the organization between congresses but met infrequently. The UUA was by far the largest financial contributor to the IARF, and by custom the UUA president occupied our denomination's seat on the council.

When I took office, I resolved not to travel overseas for at least two years. I was busy dealing with the crises in our denomination, our Association was in terrible financial condition, and my predecessor had been severely and widely criticized for excessive international travel. One of my earliest actions was to recommend to the UUA trustees that they fill our denomination's seat on the IARF council by appointing Diether Gehrmann instead of me. An ordained Unitarian Universalist minister, Gehrmann had attended universities in Germany as well as Unitarian theological schools in the United States and, at the time of my proposal, was minister of our congregation in Pomona, New York. In addition to extensive youth and adult experience in international liberal religious organizations, including the IARF, he had been minister of a large Free Religious church in Germany for ten years before returning to the United States.

As a result of our 1969 budget cuts and extensive reorganization (see the chapter "Financial Crisis and Organizational Changes"), the UUA Office of Overseas and Interfaith Relations was abolished and its responsibilities transferred to the office of the executive vice president. I proposed that the IARF also change its organizational structure by replacing the dispersed three-person secretariat with a general secretary and that a full-time professional be appointed to the position. The IARF Congress approved the change in August 1972, and the council selected Diether Gehrmann to be the first full-time general secretary in the organization's history. A financial grant from the Veatch program of our congregation in Plandome, New York (see the chapter "The Veatch Program and Holdeen Trusts") was crucial to accomplishing that significant improvement.

Gehrmann was an energetic, hardworking general secretary who focused on increasing the number and nationalities of member groups and broadening the nature and scope of IARF programs. Among key IARF achievements under his leadership were expanding the number of IARF member groups and contacts in India, Africa, and Japan and dramatically enhancing the quantity and substance of conferences, institutes, and meetings between triennial congresses. For example, during 1977 eleven IARF institutes and conferences took place in India, Belgium, Switzerland, Transylvania, England, Germany, the Netherlands, and the United States. As I left office, the IARF was a stronger and larger organization with forty-three member groups in twenty countries.

I began traveling overseas in April 1972 during my third year as president. I visited Romania, Hungary, and Czechoslovakia, and participated in the British General Assembly. My wife Nancy and I went to Transylvania, accompanied by Lajos Kovacs, bishop of the Unitarian churches in Romania. That denomination consisted of 120 Unitarian congregations in Transylvania—most of them more than four hundred years old—with eighty-five thousand members. For approximately a week, I visited churches, the Unitarian theological school, university students, and other religious officials, giving sermons in two churches and addresses on several other occasions. One day, we arose at five in the morning and visited thirteen congregations between then and midnight. From Transylvania, Nancy and I went to Budapest, where we both gave brief talks and visited with the bishop of Unitarian churches in Hungary and several congregants. During three days in Prague, a city I found depressing and menacing, our activities were confined to enjoying the company of the minister of the Czech Unitarian church and three of its key members, whom we met with individually; the government would not permit me to speak to a group.

In 1972, the UUA trustees approved my recommendation that our Association give $10 thousand from designated funds to refurbish the Unitarian theological school in Transylvania. That year I began serving as our denomination's representative on the IARF Council and as a member of the Executive Committee. During my remaining five years as UUA president, I traveled to IARF meetings in the Netherlands, England, and Germany, as well as to British General Assemblies, and I participated actively in the 1972 and 1975 IARF congresses at Heidelberg and Montreal.

Throughout those years, four IARF study commissions continued their work, which was the focal point of selected conferences and institutes. Composed of academics and scholars from various member groups, the first three commissions had been appointed in 1966 and the fourth in 1969. Their respective titles were The Christian in the World of Today; The Religious Approach to the Modern World; The Dialogue of World Religions; and Peace, Justice, and Human Rights.

The first IARF conference was held in Nigeria in 1973. The following year, the IARF moved its headquarters from The Hague to Frankfurt and initiated its partnerships program that paired local congregations in different countries to engage in cross-cultural interchanges. The first ten churches enrolled in the program were five Unitarian congregations in Romania and Hungary, matched with counterparts in New York; Boston; Dallas; Sheffield, England; and Plandome, New York. The 1976 IARF conference in Japan was titled Interreligious Dialogue: New Paths to Understanding; delegates from eight countries participated in consecutive events at the central locations of all four Japanese member groups.

As Eugene Pickett, UUA president from 1979 to 1985 and subsequently IARF president, observed in 1987, Diether Gehrmann was "the person most responsible for broadening and strengthening the Association. . . . His devotion, determination, and vision have enhanced the vitality of the IARF in many measurable ways."

When I outlined my three-year goals during the 1973 UUA General Assembly, I cited our history as a major priority area:

Today a weakness among our membership is a lack of awareness of our Unitarian Universalist history and heritage. Knowledge of our own history and heritage is essential for the continuity of our free religious movement. We need not reinvent the wheel each decade. We need not repeat mistakes of our predecessors. We should know how and why we are what we are as a free religious movement.

Lajos Kovacs, bishop of the Unitarian churches in Transylvania and IARF president, presented a relevant opportunity in 1977. A scholar who attended universities in several European countries and spoke nine languages, he was a professor of theology before he was elected bishop. I invited him to come to the United States in the spring of 1977 as a guest of our denomination, to speak about Transylvanian Unitarianism.

The UUA staff prepared posters announcing the bishop's itinerary and distributed them to individual congregations well in advance. His schedule included area meetings in Cleveland, Chicago, Minneapolis, San Francisco, Los Angeles, New Jersey, Boston, Washington, and Long Island. He also preached at Sunday services and held press conferences in New York and Boston; met with the UUA board and headquarters staff; attended the Unitarian Universalist Christian Fellowship conference in Boston; had lunch in Washington with UUA moderator Joseph Fisher and the other Unitarian Universalist members of Congress; and visited Meadville Lombard Theological School and Harvard Divinity School, receiving an honorary doctorate of humane letters from Meadville Lombard.

At each area gathering, I introduced Bishop Kovacs and moderated a lengthy discussion session after his address. At the conclusion of those four eventful weeks, it was clear from all our experiences that the objectives of his visit had been achieved: enhanced awareness and deeper knowledge of our history and heritage as well as strengthened bonds with present-day members of those sixteenth-century Unitarian churches in central Europe.

Professional Religious Leadership

IN CONTRAST TO THE longstanding fellowship process for certifying ministers, the UUA lacked a procedure to establish standards or ascertain qualifications for directors of religious education until 1968. Our directors had formed a voluntary professional organization, the Liberal Religious Education Directors Association (LREDA). The standards for admission to LREDA were a college degree and two years experience as a paid religious education director of a congregation. Thus, the standards for entering the Unitarian Universalist religious education profession—other than the college degree requirement—were determined by the committee or board of a single congregation.

In 1968, a hundred of our churches had church school enrollments of more than 250 children, yet there were only sixty-nine professional religious education directors serving in our denomination. Making the situation worse, no more than a dozen professional directors were willing to change their place of residence; most were women who wished to live in the area where their husbands worked. By early 1968, however, the Division of Education and Board of Trustees succeeded in creating a mechanism to establish standards and certification procedures for professional directors as well as to implement recruiting and training. The board appointed a certifying committee to function in a manner similar to the UUA Fellowship Committee that accredited ministers, and in February 1968 the new committee announced the standards for accrediting UUA professional religious education directors.

The new standards included personal, experience, and education requirements. Among the experience qualifications were classroom teaching of preschool, elementary, and adolescent children, plus at least two years' administration of a Unitarian Universalist church school that included an approved amount of experience in adult and parent education, training and supervision of teachers, and worship. Education requirements entailed a general acquaintance with the sciences and humanities, accompanied by working knowledge in the areas of education, religion, psychology, liberal religious education, and communication skills. Prerequisites in those five areas included more than twenty specific subjects.

Although a graduate or college degree was encouraged to facilitate meeting education requirements, the program was designed to enable a person with two years of college to work in a church school, take academic courses, attend institutes, and thus meet the requirements for accreditation. Each study program leading to certification was tailored for the individual. A qualified person of the candidate's choice was assigned as a mentor to determine a study program, which had to be accomplished within four years, and to counsel the candidate throughout.

By the fall of 1971, sixteen people had completed the program of accreditation. Twenty-five candidates were in training, and another dozen were about to embark on their courses of study. The UUA accreditation program not only served to improve the quality of religious education leadership in our denomination, it also formed the basis for much of the work of subsequent committees during the 1970s concerning the education and certification of all Unitarian Universalist professional religious leaders.

Ministerial Education Commission

In January 1972, I proposed that the UUA board create a six-member Ministerial Education Commission (MEC). Every year I had to make budget recommendations to the Finance Committee, specifying the amounts to be allocated to each of the three ministerial schools most closely associated with our denomination—Meadville Lombard in Chicago; Starr King in Berkeley, California; and Harvard Divinity in Cambridge, Massachusetts. Then the Finance Committee and subsequently the entire board went through similar decision-making processes. I believed that the board, Finance Committee, and I did not know enough about what each of the schools was doing, that we needed help to make informed decisions. I also thought such a commission could serve to upgrade the quality of professional education for our religious leadership and might well generate recommendations for needed changes that were not readily apparent in the existing conventional wisdom within our denomination.

The trustees readily appointed the commission and designated Carl Scovel, minister of King's Chapel in Boston, as chairperson. The MEC mandate from the board was straightforward: to make recommendations to the UUA administration regarding annual budget allocations related to support of education for professional religious leadership, to solicit and allocate money from various sources to support such education, and to follow "the criterion of improving the quality of education for our professional religious leadership."

Four months later, the MEC made a preliminary report affirming that it would focus on improving preparation for local parish ministries, which included religious education directors. "We are concerned with preparation, that is, with academic and nonacademic educational experience, and with the financing and structuring of those educational experiences," the MEC announced. It had not begun soliciting and allocating funds, as it believed it must first conduct limited research and prepare proposals in four areas: articulating a core educational experience, enunciating criteria and means for awarding scholarship aid, developing recommendations about aspects of the accreditation process related to preparation for the parish ministry, and improving opportunities for the continuing education of parish ministers.

In its January 1973 progress report, the commission reported on the costs and income sources for UUA-related theological schools, as well as records of their graduates, for the past eleven years. The report included several observations about theological education in our denomination, among them that our two Unitarian Universalist schools (Meadville Lombard and Starr King) had no direct responsibility to the UUA and that increasing numbers of our seminarians were studying at non-Unitarian Universalist schools. The commission also stated, "We are too small a denomination and our resources are too limited for the UUA to commit itself to support seminaries." The only specific recommendations in the report pertained to UUA direct funding of theological schools: that the board end all such funding by the summer of 1976, announce a moratorium on all funding for ministerial education until after receiving the commission's full proposals later in 1973, and amend UUA policy to let Starr King engage in unrestricted fundraising as Meadville Lombard and Harvard were permitted to do.

The MEC presented another progress report to the board that March. After indicating its intention to submit a full set of recommendations in October, the commission identified four key points on which its members agreed:

(1) We need ministers who are intellectually strong, professionally able, personally integrated, and religiously aware.
(2) Education for the ministry is a lifelong process; continuing education is fully as important as seminary education.
(3) We find no single school that is training our future ministers in the fourfold adequacy we describe in point one.
(4) It is the responsibility of the Unitarian Universalist Association to make sure its ministers are fully trained and continuously educated.

The commission reported that it had completed visits to Meadville Lombard, Starr King, and Harvard Divinity, and spent at least three days in each school "visiting classes, talking with faculty and administration, with students, with alumni, and where possible with board members. We have studied the curricula and the teaching schedules; we have studied the records of the graduates; and we have performed, we believe, as exhaustive an analysis of these three schools as has been made for our denomination in at least the last fifteen years." The report noted that the percentage of our ministerial students enrolled at non-Unitarian Universalist seminaries had increased from 15 percent to 41 percent in the last four years.

In April 1973, the commission sent a brief questionnaire to all Unitarian Universalist ministers asking about the nature of their educational experiences since graduation from seminary, the kind of education they believed they would need in the future, and how the UUA could help them get that education.

The Executive Committee of the Unitarian Universalist Ministers Association (UUMA) passed a resolution that summer urging UUA trustees to refrain from taking action on the commission's forthcoming October report until the April 1974 board meeting. The resolution observed that "it is an intense issue capable of arousing deep and divided feelings in ministers and churches alike," and noted that the majority of UUMA chapters would not meet until the coming winter and spring to have an opportunity to understand and discuss policies the commission might recommend. The UUMA statement declared that policies affecting ministerial education "must be implemented with the intelligent and informed good will of most of the ministers" if they are to be workable.

In October, the MEC submitted its report to the board, which promptly distributed copies to all congregations. The report pointed out,

> The UUA has created six Ministerial Education Commissions in the twelve years of its existence. This has happened

because responsibility for ministerial education has not been clearly defined and built into the existing UUA structure. The fact that new committees were continually appointed and could not meet the ongoing and changing needs for ministerial education only shows that this responsibility cannot be avoided. Money must be apportioned, new directions must be ventured, old ones reevaluated, and someone must make and implement these decisions.

The commission emphasized its belief that "the UUA's paramount need is for a single responsible, permanent instrument with the power to make and implement decisions affecting ministerial education."

Much of the report was devoted to conveying the commission's views and recommendations concerning a core curriculum and internships for people in training, continuing education for those in service, theological school programs and regional institutes for ministers as well as students, special summer institutes, and a Center for Religious Leadership. In the introduction to its description of internships, the MEC said that while the seminary may well be designed to offer courses, seminars, and tutorials in both academic and practical areas, the best professional training is an intensive personal experience under a competent, experienced supervisor in a local parish setting.

The commission proposed a Unitarian Universalist Center for Religious Leadership as a long-range goal:

> We envision a Center becoming a place of UU educational identity . . . a place for the study of both practical and academic subjects of significance to UUs, for the publication of significant religious pamphlets or articles, for the study and practice of those spiritual disciplines which commend themselves to free religious societies. The Center should have access to a good library of Unitarian Universalist materials, as well as proximity to a metropolis with good cultural and educational resources.

To implement its recommendations, the MEC proposed a seven-member Council on Ministerial Education and a director of ministerial education. The council's responsibilities were to secure funds from the UUA budget and other sources, decide how the money would be spent, evaluate existing ministerial education programs, explore new ventures in ministerial education, advise the director on priorities, and consult on academic and professional standards with the UUA Ministerial Fellowship Committee, which had responsibility for accrediting Unitarian Universalist ministers. The director of ministerial education would be an associate director in the UUA Department of Ministry.

As an immediate board action, the MEC recommended that the trustees promptly give wide distribution to the commission's October report and invite discussion and feedback. For the April 1974 board meeting, the MEC recommended that the trustees approve the October report with such amendments as the commission might add, begin a search for the new director of ministerial education, dissolve the MEC, approve the proposed budget for the new ministerial education council, and appoint the council as a permanent standing committee.

Following additional consultations with professional religious leaders throughout the denomination, the commission reported to the board on criticisms of four MEC proposals: the Center for Religious Leadership, the Council on Ministerial Education, internships, and terminating direct UUA funding for Starr King school. There was also criticism of the commission's statement that it "found no school that we believe is adequately preparing our ministers for the fourfold standard of ministry we have enunciated."

In response to the last criticism, the MEC apologized and acknowledged that adequately was at best an unfortunate word in that it "implied total failure rather than an incompleteness." The commission pointed out, however, that not all responses to its recommendations were negative: There was also genuine and strong support, including positive reactions from a number of ministers as well as the UUA committees responsible for accrediting ministers and religious education directors.

The commission emphasized in its January 1974 report that at the heart of the MEC recommendations was the proposal for a council whose members would be accountable to the UUA board for the use of Association monies in implementing ministerial education. The commission reaffirmed its proposal for an intensive internship experience but dropped the proposal for a ministerial education center, mainly because it had been "consistently misunderstood" to be a school with a permanent faculty. The MEC also withdrew its proposal to phase out direct UUA funding of Starr King and made one new recommendation: that the board appoint a committee to explore the possibility of merging ministers and religious education directors in regard to their education and accreditation at whatever levels seemed feasible.

The commission, presenting its final report to the board in April 1974, acknowledged that even its remaining recommendations were controversial. "But we believe controversy is not necessarily an argument against our proposal. It . . . means change, we believe for the better, while preserving the best of our present practices."

In the end, the trustees did not approve the MEC report. The board postponed consideration indefinitely, but it did vote to approve a 1974 budget allocation for Starr King and permit the school to engage in general fundraising for operating purposes, authorize an immediate search for a director of ministerial education, appoint at its October 1974 meeting a special committee to explore the possibility of merging ministers and religious education directors in regard to their education and accreditation, and dismiss the Ministerial Education Commission. The trustees instructed the moderator to appoint a board committee to draft alternative proposals for a Council on Ministerial Education, to be considered along with those recommended in the MEC report.

Within six weeks, Eugene Pickett, who subsequently served as UUA president from 1979 to 1985, was appointed director of ministerial education. In June 1974, the board created a Council on

Education for Professional Religious Leadership, whose responsibilities included recommending an annual ministerial education budget to the board, securing funds for ministerial education, evaluating ministerial education programs, exploring new ventures in ministerial education, and advising the director of ministerial education. All seven council members had been appointed by January 1975. In April 1977—after receiving the final report of the special committee charged with exploring the possibility of merging ministers and religious education directors in regard to their education and accreditation—the board approved the recommendations in principle and voted to recognize two forms of ministry, parish and education.

After the Ministerial Education Commission's labors had run their course in 1974, many of its members were disappointed and discouraged. They noted in retrospect that of their original key proposals, only the internships recommendation came to fruition, and the council the UUA board created wasn't given the authority to do what was required. Members believed that the theological schools had perceived them as adversaries. Some MEC members have acknowledged that they should have done a better job of educating and informing ministers during the two years of their work, and that in hindsight they underestimated the financial straits of the UUA, which probably made the center and council proposals appear unrealistic.

I don't share a pessimistic view. Though the commission didn't succeed in achieving the whole of what it sought, its hard work resulted in changes for the better within our denomination. The types of internships it recommended were instituted, a continuing seven-member Council on Education for Professional Religious Leadership came into being with most of the proposed responsibilities, the UUA appointed a director of ministerial education, and our Association began to recognize two forms of ministry—parish and education—thus merging ministers and religious education directors in regard to their education and accreditation. But just as, or even more, important was the light the commission focused on the standards, practices, and financing of professional education in our denomination, which enabled progress in succeeding years. I continue to be grateful for the demonstrated dedication and difficult labors of the commission members.

Two major related developments during my tenure were the increasing numbers of women preparing for our ministry and of Unitarian Universalist ministerial students studying at non-Unitarian Universalist seminaries. In 1974, when the MEC presented its final report, 43 percent of our seminarians were enrolled in non-Unitarian Universalist schools, compared to 15 percent five years earlier. There was no simple reason. Many such schools apparently had become sufficiently liberal for our students to study there profitably. The Unitarian Universalist ministerial students who responded to a 1973 questionnaire cited reputation, financial considerations, and location as their reasons for attending those seminaries. Most respondents hadn't applied for admission to Meadville Lombard, Starr King, or Harvard Divinity.

The number of women in our ministry increased remarkably beginning in the early seventies. In the summer of 1969, the UUA Ministerial Fellowship Committee interviewed seventeen candidates, all of them men; among the thirteen candidates considered in mid-1977, eight were women. From 1969 through 1971, our Association received two women into ministerial fellowship each year, yet in 1972 we welcomed six as new ministers, and nine the final year of my tenure. The increase continued during subsequent years and also applied to the number of women holding active ministerial positions.

Another sign of the trend was the total number of women who were in fellowship as accredited Unitarian Universalist ministers: The total was thirty-three in 1972 and grew to sixty in 1977. The demographics of ministerial school enrollment also reflected progress: In 1973 there were twenty-one women studying for our ministry and by 1977 the number was seventy-three—half our total ministerial student population. The early and middle seventies were a turning point in the number of women preparing for and serving in active ministerial positions.

During that period, the UUA Department of Ministry continued to perform its essential day-to-day functions assisting our congregations and professional religious leaders, despite severe financial and staff constrictions. The department was closely involved in the developments mentioned earlier in this chapter, as well as in ministerial settlement, interim ministers, and ministerial finances.

One of the innovations necessitated by the 1969 financial crisis and consequent reorganization was that every district had a ministerial settlement representative, a qualified volunteer whose expenses were reimbursed by the UUA, to provide local assistance to congregations seeking new ministers. The Department of Ministry appointed each of the twenty-three representatives in consultation with the districts they served. Initially, representatives were authorized to make only one visit to churches seeking to fill ministerial vacancies; beginning in 1975, however, the number of visits increased to three. Other improvements in the mid-seventies were a revised ministerial settlement manual, expanded UUA resources for congregations involved in the search process, a yearly training conference for all settlement representatives, strengthened confidentiality for the search process, and enhanced procedures for securing reliable information and interviewing potential candidates.

Interim Ministries

An interim minister serves a congregation between the departure of a settled minister and the arrival of a successor. In the early seventies, there were at most only a half-dozen interim ministries in our denomination at any one time, and they were perceived by the congregations and ministers as primarily performing maintenance or caretaker functions. That changed in 1976 when the Department of Ministry, in cooperation with a group of clergy, held the first training event for interim ministers and launched an accredited interim-ministry program that continues to this day. At the core of the program was a new concept of interim ministers that incorporated the roles of consultative specialists and change agents. Other aspects were explicit standards, yearly performance reviews, continuing education, shared learnings from field experiences, and annual seminars. The number of interim ministries soon more than doubled, reflecting greater awareness among our congregations of benefits derived from specialists trained to help them through ministerial transitions.

Council on Ministerial Finances

The mid-seventies also saw the creation of a Council on Ministerial Finances to coordinate and enhance ministerial financial-aid programs and benefits, improve financial counsel for ministers, and provide resources for congregations concerning ministerial salaries and benefits. The new body comprised representatives from the Department of Ministry, Unitarian Universalist Ministers Association, Liberal Religious Education Directors Association, Unitarian Universalist Women's Federation, Unitarian Pension Society, Society for Ministerial Relief, and Universalist Convention of New York. The council assumed responsibility for what had been known as "ministerial welfare," which included administering aid funds for active and retired ministers and their families. In 1976, the UUA established the full-time position of director for ministerial finances, further strengthening financial counsel for ministers and churches.

Licensed Lay Leadership

In the early seventies, a number of people put forth the view that our denomination should have a program to license lay ministers or certify lay leaders. The UUA Ministerial Fellowship Committee responded by undertaking a lengthy examination of the feasibility and advisability of such a program. The most serious deliberations centered on a paraprofessional role for lay leaders that required preparation and credentials. The committee put forth its proposal in 1974 but soon withdrew it pending further study. In the spring of 1975, the committee tabled all proposals to establish such a program. One stated reason was continuing negative reactions from the Accreditation Committee for Religious Education Directors, which was concerned about appropriate training and credentials; a significant number of ministers who objected on similar grounds, many citing their experience in the Universalist Church of America, where the practice tended to weaken small congregations; and districts concerned about the confusion and inequities that could stem from having too many models with varying standards and requirements. The committee also believed that "it would be unwise to add another category of religious leadership at this time," and that the group was "not capable of presenting a plan that would gain widespread acceptance" at that juncture.

The MEC was right that we need religious leaders who are intellectually strong, professionally able, personally integrated, and religiously aware, and that our Association has the responsibility to make sure they are fully trained and continuously educated. Such leaders are a necessity if our religious movement is to continue as a viable entity, effective in the lives of our congregations' members as well as in the general culture. The issues permeating how best to accomplish that will be with us continually as we endeavor to maintain the high standards that were instrumental in bringing our denomination into being and are essential to assuring its future strength.

Associate Organizations

THE UUA TRUSTEES approve associate member status for certain major independent organizations whose purposes and programs are auxiliary to and supportive of our Association's principles. In 1969, five organizations were UUA associate members: the Women's Federation, Service Committee, Liberal Religious Youth, Student Religious Liberals, and Laymen's League. By 1972, there were two additional associate members: the Black Affairs Council and Black and White Action. All seven still were associate members when I left office in 1977. Other organizations approved by the board for affiliate status with the Association were known as affiliate members.

Black and White Action

Black and White Action (BAWA), came into being as an alternative to the "blacks only" approach for remedying racial ills that was advocated by the Black Unitarian Universalist Caucus (BUUC) and the Black Affairs Council (BAC). It became the heated focus of our highly polarized 1968 and 1969 General Assemblies (see the chapters "Black UU Caucus and Black Affairs Council" and "Black UU Caucus Court Proceedings").

The purpose of BAWA, as described in one of its leaflets, was to be a forceful Unitarian Universalist presence in the ongoing struggle to help "all those who are submerged in our society, whether they be black or white or red or brown, to emerge into full participation in the opportunities and responsibilities of the American mainstream." Members of BAWA believed that people of different races could and should work together toward achieving those objectives. BAWA opposed the separatist approach that BUUC advocated yet never opposed the existence of BUUC. In the words of BAWA co-chair Max Gaebler, "What we did oppose was their insistence that theirs was the only way and there was no place for us." Other top officers of BAWA from its earliest days were co-chair Glover Barnes and executive secretary Betty Seiden.

BAWA members, black and white, experienced profound pain and disillusionment when the 1968 and 1969 UUA General Assemblies voted not only to give $1 million to the separatist BAC but also to specifically prohibit the UUA from contributing any funds to BAWA. Additionally, members of BAWA were dismayed by the verbal abuse directed at them by those who disagreed with their integrationist approach. But BAWA did not dissolve after 1968 and 1969. The group continued its programs, as well as its dialogue with the UUA board and denomination at large.

The 1970 and 1971 General Assemblies affirmed the board decisions that our Association would no longer contribute funds to BAC from UUA annual budgets, having donated $450 thousand in 1968 and 1969. It was obvious prior to and during the 1971 General Assembly that Unitarian Universalists were deeply divided about whether contributions for furthering racial justice should be given to either BAC or BAWA. Ultimately the delegates passed a resolution declaring that "denominational division and polarization on the issue of how best to fight racism have gone on long enough, therefore the General Assembly desires a single, joint fundraising campaign to finance all Unitarian Universalist efforts (other than the Unitarian Universalist Service Committee) to achieve racial justice." The UUA board and administration were directed to "confer with BAC, BAWA, and all other interested parties to implement such united fundraising."

After six months of strenuous striving, the UUA board regretfully concluded that none of the proposed joint fundraising arrangements was acceptable to all the major entities involved. Three months later, the Veatch program gave $250 thousand to the Association for a special fund to promote racial justice and combat racism, specifying that the UUA allocate $45 thousand to BAWA. In May 1972, the administering committee of the fund contributed that sum to BAWA, reporting to the UUA board that it "found both the BAC and BAWA philosophies to be respectable approaches to racial justice and not necessarily in competition." During the 1972 General Assembly, the UUA board voted unanimously to approve BAWA as an associate member of the UUA. In 1974, the fund made additional allocations to BAWA.

The pages of the *UU World* newspaper reflect BAWA activities throughout the years of my presidency: programs, conferences, writings, annual meetings, news items, articles, letters to the editor, advertisements, fundraising, and so forth. In 1972, BAWA established the Ministry for Human Dignity and Social Change, appointing Dan Higgins the minister. The purpose was to provide a denominational pulpit as a forum to address the polarity in the UUA about black empowerment; the BAWA directors believed a dialogue was possible because the intensity of polarization had diminished. The minister also worked with local BAWA chapters, directed BAWA projects, and developed continental BAWA programs in cooperation with the Leadership Conference on Civil Rights, Project Equality, and other groups working toward an integrated society.

One BAWA program produced and distributed TV spots on topics such as our common humanity and the relevance of minority histories to United States history. There were numerous BAWA events in various locations across the continent, often featuring nationally known speakers and public officials. The organization continued to be a significant presence during UUA general assemblies: The largest event at the 1977 General Assembly was the BAWA lecture given by Arthur Fleming, chairman of the U.S. Civil Rights Commission.

Women's Federation

The Unitarian Universalist Women's Federation (UUWF) came into being in 1963 as a consolidation of the Alliance of Unitarian Women, founded in 1890, and the Association of Universalist Women, formed in 1869. No group was more understanding or supportive of the UUA during our crisis period. The organization accepted without complaint the reductions in financial support from the UUA and performed a continually constructive role as our denomination moved through those difficult years. I was and continue to be deeply grateful to the UUWF as an organization and to the individual women who were leaders and members during that time.

The Women's Federation was a strong and pervasive presence in our religious movement, regularly using the *UU World* newspaper to reach Unitarian Universalist women across the continent. The UUWF published multiple-page inserts in issue after issue to convey information about its programs, positions, and activities, as well as events in our denomination and the world related to women's concerns. The organization, which had numerous local chapters in all regions of the continent, was also active in denominational affairs, sending representatives to UUA board meetings, advocating UUWF positions during General Assemblies, and throughout the years encouraging widespread discussion of denominational concerns that intersected with its own.

The Women's Federation was active in promoting feminism and pursuing equal participation of women in all aspects of our society and denomination. In 1970, the Federation sponsored, and Beacon Press published, *Voices of the New Feminism* by Mary Lou MacDonald. The UUWF similarly joined with the UUA in publishing *Self Discovery: Group Explorations in Life Crises*.

In 1972, the Women's Federation presented to the General Assembly a resolution that called for eliminating discriminatory masculine language from the UUA bylaws, specifically, removing pronouns designating gender. A technicality involving its submission prevented the assembly from voting on the proposal, and I promised the delegates that I would instruct UUA counsel to prepare such bylaw changes for action at the next General Assembly. The amendments were approved in 1973.

In a similar vein, responding to a comment from a UUWF leader, I worked with UUA counsel to change the criteria for recipients of Stanfield scholarships. The scholarships—funded through a trust created by Mrs. Marion Barr Stanfield and named for her and her husband Otto, members of the Unitarian church in Westport, Connecticut—were awarded annually by the UUA to Unitarian Universalists studying in the fields of art or law, with special consideration given to beneficiaries "most likely to use their legal training and their training in art for the betterment of humankind." The provisions of the trust specified that art scholarships be awarded to females and law scholarships to males. In October 1976, however, I reported to the UUA trustees that our lawyer had been successful in obtaining an order from probate court that Stanfield scholarships for both art and law could be awarded to male or female recipients.

In 1974, the UUWF established the Ministry to Women award, which was presented at annual UUA General Assemblies to an individual or organization who had ministered to women in an outstanding manner.

Service Committee

The Unitarian Universalist Service Committee (UUSC) was formed in 1963 by the merger of the Unitarian Service Committee, established in 1940, and the Universalist Service Committee, formed in 1945. Both organizations performed humanitarian work in Europe during World War II.

As the separate denominations neared their 1961 consolidation, the Unitarians had two social responsibility operations, the autonomous Unitarian Service Committee and an active Department of Social Responsibility that was part of Unitarian headquarters. The Universalist Service Committee functioned as the social responsibility department of Universalist headquarters. Whether to implement the Universalist or Unitarian model within the consolidated denomination was such a contentious issue that the matter wasn't decided until two years after our formal merger. The Unitarian version prevailed; the UUSC emerged as an autonomous organization, yet UUA headquarters included a Department of Social Responsibility.

The UUSC had, and has today, a variety of programs and activities with the overarching aims of promoting social justice and human rights throughout the world, supporting struggles of oppressed groups, and responding strategically to disasters. Funded primarily by voluntary contributions from individuals, the Service Committee also receives financial support from congregations and foundations. During my initial years in office, the UUSC accepted some financial support from the government. However, an intense controversy arose concerning a Service Committee project that involved training social workers to help inhabitants in Vietnamese villages, for which the organization had received financing from a U.S. government entity, the Agency for International Development (AID). After consequent protests from Unitarian Universalist members that included a sit-in at UUSC headquarters in Boston, the Service Committee withdrew from the AID contract in February 1971 and no longer accepts financial support from the federal government.

Some representative UUSC programs and activities during my tenure were a community health program in Togo; assistance for clergy in El Salvador to publish a self-help and literacy newsletter for the poor; a community center in Houston that provided legal, educational, and community services to Chicanos; active participation in the National Moratorium on Prison Construction, which sought alternatives to incarceration as well as other criminal justice reforms; an all-Caribbean conference on family planning and community development; and a fact-finding tour to El Salvador that culminated in UUSC representatives testifying before the House International Relations Committee.

In view of the overlapping focus of the UUSC and the UUA Department of Education and Social Concern, the UUA trustees appointed a seven-person joint committee in 1973 to clarify their roles and relationship. The committee was composed of a UUA vice moderator as chair and an equal number of members—staff and trustees—from each of the two organizations. The main proposal considered was that the UUSC assume the social responsibility functions of the UUA Department of Education and Social Concern; retain the current UUSC name, Board of Trustees, staff organization, and fundraising capabilities; and have an institutional relationship to the UUA similar to that of Beacon Press. In effect, the Service Committee would become the denomination's continental arm for social action and the existing department would drop "social concern" from its name and functions.

After months of deliberation, the joint committee recommended, with one dissenting vote, that the above proposal be implemented. The UUA board favored the recommendation, but we were informed in October 1974 that the UUSC board had rejected it. I expressed my regret that the action of the Service Committee trustees prevented the proposal from being considered by the numerous UUSC members in Unitarian Universalist congregations.

However, the UUA and the Service Committee continued to cooperate. For example, in March 1975, the two organizations established a jointly administered hunger relief fund. Contributions to the fund were divided equally between the UUSC and the UUA.

Youth Organizations

Our continental Unitarian Universalist youth groups also were associate members of the UUA: Liberal Religious Youth (LRY) was the high-school-age organization and Student Religious Liberals (SRL) was the college-age group. Leaders of both, especially those of college age, were caught up in the late-1960s and early-1970s atmosphere of demonstrations, anti-institutionalism, and confrontation. Even before I was president, back when I was a member of

the Education Advisory Committee, the UUA seemed to be continually adjusting its arrangements with our continental youth
groups, trying to cope with the new phases of youth culture as
they emerged.

In 1971, the UUA board voted to discontinue regular financial
contributions to the two youth groups and instead allocate $50
thousand for youth programs to be administered by the UUA
Department of Education with a Youth Advisory Committee. The
board also gave sufficient funds to the youth organizations to hold
their annual meetings and develop proposals to be funded from
the yearly $50-thousand allocation.

Four years later, SRL voted not to accept money from the
UUA Youth Advisory Committee. The committee proceeded to
appoint a coordinator of college-level programs, whose responsibilities were to develop communication and programs among
young adult Unitarian Universalists. The new college-level program replaced SRL as a participant in Youth Advisory Committee
deliberations.

In 1976, after listening to presentations from leaders of LRY
and the college-level programs, the UUA board established a
Special Committee on Youth Programs. The committee was
charged with studying our denomination's youth programs, with
a view to developing and budgeting new and better ways to meet
the needs of liberal religious young people.

Later that year, SRL advised the UUA that it wanted to be
known as SRL, a Free Religious Fellowship; the group said that its
new direction reflected the collective living movement and that it
wished to maintain ties with the Association. The UUA board
voted to continue the status of SRL as an associate member.

Laymen's League

During the first fifteen years following its founding in 1919, the
Unitarian Universalist Laymen's League was the major fundraising
arm of the American Unitarian Association. In the early decades

of its existence, the league was a strong organization, with chapters in congregations and cities across the continent, and a variety of programs and activities; it became smaller and weaker in the years just prior to my election. For many years, a trademark of the group was its nationally published advertisements that asked, "Are you a Unitarian Universalist without knowing it?"

In 1974, the league leadership approved a reorganization that included retaining an executive vice president. The group's stated purpose was to support our Association by working closely with the UUA "through its pilot projects, for the extension of liberal religion on the American continent." Besides various other activities, the league produced and made available to congregations and districts a series of brief radio spots advertising Unitarian Universalist religion, designed for broadcast on local stations. In 1976, the organization raised $10 thousand for the UUA committee on aging. After celebrating its sixtieth anniversary in 1978, the league legally dissolved in June 1979.

The special recognition of certain major organizations as associate members is a reminder that our denomination is a family of organizations, formed and sustained by Unitarian Universalists, whose purposes are auxiliary to and supportive of one another's. The years have demonstrated that together the members of this family can accomplish far more to fulfill those purposes and advance their ideals than they can apart.

UUA Offices

COMPLEMENTING THE programs of UUA associate organizations were several offices with connections to UUA headquarters, each with distinctive purposes, programs, and activities. Some existed at the time I was elected and others originated while I was in office; nearly all underwent changes that engendered controversy during my presidency. A common thread was the necessity to adhere to our UUA financial and program priorities and allocate our diminished resources in a balanced manner.

United Nations Office

More than eighty years ago, Unitarians and Universalists were active in the League of Nations Association, and two decades later they were intensely interested in the founding of the United Nations, which they actively supported throughout the 1950s. When the two denominations consolidated in 1961, the UUA board appointed a United Nations advisory committee. In April 1962, UN ambassador Adlai Stevenson suggested that each of our congregations appoint an envoy "to promote better knowledge and understanding of the United Nations." He said all Unitarian Universalists had the opportunity to "help us build a better world." Acting on his words, volunteers immediately established the first UU-UN Office, working in space provided by the Community Church of New York Unitarian Universalist.

In 1969, the UUA was allocating approximately $21 thousand annually to the UU-UN Office, and its director was a staff member in the UUA Department of Social Responsibility. As part of budget reductions, the staff member was terminated and the allocation reduced to $4,300 (equivalent to about $24.5 thousand today). In January 1970, after noting that the UN Advisory Committee was raising funds to retain office staff, the UUA board approved a plan whereby a UUA staff member would be appointed director of the UN Office and the Advisory Committee would become the United Nations Committee and responsible to the UUA board and president. At the June trustees' meeting, I reported that the UN Committee had decided instead to become a voluntary organization supported by voluntary contributions and have an affiliate relationship with the UUA similar to that of the former Unitarian Universalist Fellowship for Social Justice. The UU-UN Office began placing regular "window on the world" advertisements in our denominational newspaper, inviting individuals, congregations, and groups to enroll as voluntary members. In 1972, a Continental Clergy Committee launched a promotional campaign for an emergency offering on United Nations Sunday in all our congregations to help maintain the office after direct financial support from the UUA budget ended.

The UU-UN Office continues to this day as an associate member of the UUA and our denomination's voice at the United Nations. With its staff located at the church center across from UN headquarters, a major function of the office is education—informing Unitarian Universalists across the continent about how they can help the UN be more effective, conducting seminars and youth conferences at the UN, and sponsoring United Nations Sundays in our congregations.

At our Association's 1971 annual UN seminar, I gave the keynote address, "The Unitarian Universalist Stake in the World Community." My opening statement was,

For all of us in the Unitarian Universalist movement, the cause of a world community is not a pious wish—it is a vital necessity. The vision of a world that is a genuine community of persons and of nations is a vision we all share. It is a vision that continually challenges us to work for change, even at times when we may be weary or worried or afraid.

After reviewing the historical concept of world community in our denomination, I posed the question: What is at stake in world community?

All we believe in as Unitarian Universalists is at stake . . . our faith, our dreams, our lives. If in our time the faith of some seems to falter, if today we may be less sure of success, if now we seem less certain that the old promises will be fulfilled, we yet must continue. All of us know how dark and dangerous is this time in human history—no one would deny it. Perhaps the very density of the darkness will cause more persons to kindle lights. We must continue to work for world community. Because we are who we are, we can do no other.

Two months before I left office in 1977, I was privileged to be a guest at a UN luncheon honoring the presidents of voluntary organizations affiliated with the United Nations Association, at which Secretary General Kurt Waldheim and other UN officials spoke.

Washington Office for Social Concern

At the time I was elected in 1969, we were operating a full-time Washington office as part of the UUA Department of Social Responsibility. Its functions were to represent to the U.S. Congress and administration our denomination's stated positions on legislative and public policy matters, work in cooperation with other religious bodies to have our voices heard at the highest levels of government, disseminate relevant information to our congregations, and mobilize Unitarian Universalists for effective action on key issues.

Although the financial crisis I inherited necessitated a 40 percent budget cut and drastic reductions in UUA staff, we were able to retain the Washington office with a full-time director. I negotiated with leaders of the American Ethical Union and the American Humanist Association to establish the Joint Washington Office for Social Concern as a cooperative effort. Our agreement provided that the UUA would pay half the total costs of operating the office and each of the other participants would contribute one-quarter. We also agreed that any of the three organizations could change the arrangement or withdraw upon giving six month's notice.

The joint office proved to be a successful endeavor in cooperation and sharing, and in early 1973, the groups renewed their agreement for another three-year period. About two years later, however, the Humanist association notified us that it would pay only half its negotiated share in 1975. Because the Ethical Union strongly believed the UUA should contribute no more than half the total financial support, so as not to dominate the joint operation, the Humanists' action placed our shared enterprise in jeopardy.

Though we held several meetings trying to resolve the situation, in March 1975, the presidents of the three organizations jointly announced the termination of the Washington office in June: "For various reasons the three presidents have agreed that it would be in the best interest of all three organizations to discontinue their participation in the Joint Washington Office for Social Concern. . . . We take this action regretably." Concurrently I stated that "in accord with the 1975–76 budget approved by the UUA Board in January, the UUA will continue to have representation in Washington. The details of its exact nature are yet to be determined."

The UUA board and I were intent on maintaining a Washington Office for Social Concern. The UUA signed a lease for the same space occupied by the joint office, and we made arrangements to staff the office on an interim basis with a recently graduated minister and a ministerial student intern. When the board subsequently increased the amount allocated for the Washington office, we were able to employ a full-time director. The office has continued to the present and is known today as the UUA Washington Office for Advocacy.

Office of Gay Concerns

Among the controversial issues in our denomination during my two terms was establishing an Office of Gay Concerns as part of UUA headquarters. However, gay concerns were not new to the programs of our Association when the 1974 General Assembly urged the board to fund such an office: The UUA administration, Department of Ministry, and Department of Education and Social Concern had long been engaged in efforts to eliminate discrimination and prejudice against gay people and to promote understanding and equality.

The UUA curriculum *About Your Sexuality* (see the chapter "Publishing") and award-winning *The Invisible Minority* were examples. In 1972, the UUA Department of Education and Social Concern purchased the publication rights to a three-part filmstrip-record series titled *The Invisible Minority: The Homosexuals in our Society* and published the program with the full support of the UUA administration. The first part focused on the changing view of homosexuality; the second, understanding homosexuality; and the third, questions and answers concerning the homosexual way of life. The department intended the program to be used on its own or as a supplement to *About Your Sexuality*. Our *Invisible Minority* unit subsequently received an award as the best filmstrip-record educational program published in 1973, winning first place in the annual competition sponsored by the National Council on Family Relations. The UUA program was one of twenty-four entries, some of them from major producers of filmstrip-record programs, such as Time-Life of New York.

The 1973 General Assembly voted that the board should establish an Office of Gay Concerns at UUA headquarters, to be funded by sources outside the denominational budget, and specified that should such financial sources be unavailable, the UUA would not be responsible for funding the office. At its October meeting, the board voted to establish the office at UUA headquarters as requested by the General Assembly, to be part of the Department of Education and Social Concern. The board also approved guidelines for the office; its function was to be an education and program resource toward the goals of eliminating discrimination and prejudice against homosexual people; promoting understanding and equality of treatment; and fostering equal opportunity for homosexuals politically, socially, and economically. The guidelines emphasized that "it shall be clear that the function of the office is not advocacy or promotion of homosexuality as a lifestyle" and stated that the UUA "shall have no responsibility for establishing or maintaining the office unless funding is received from outside the UUA budget." The board also reiterated that UUA fundraisers were not to raise money for the office but were available "to assist the Unitarian Universalist Gay Caucus in developing sources of funding outside the UUA budget for the office and its programs."

In January 1974, I reported to the board that the director of the UUA Department of Education and Social Concern had met with members of the caucus concerning the proposed office; the UUA had received only $200 in designated contributions toward establishing the office; no one had approached the UUA fundraising office or the *UU World* newspaper for help in starting a campaign for funds; and the UUA administration remained ready to cooperate with the caucus about fundraising for the office.

That April, the board directed the UUA staff to create a model of the office, which the board approved in June. During the subsequent 1974 General Assembly, the delegates voted 376 to 311 to urge the UUA board to establish the office at UUA headquarters by using $38.5 thousand from the grants section of the UUA annual budget—specifically by eliminating the amount for religious education research and reducing the allocation for publicity and radio/television. In October, the board, by a vote of 12 to 11, decided to fund the Office of Gay Concerns at UUA headquarters as urged by the General assembly.

In a November 15 front-page *UU World* editorial, I noted that my clear recommendations to the board in October 1973 and October 1974 were that the office not be established as part of UUA headquarters. I believed the establishment of such a UUA office to be a distortion of our priorities:

> We have a wide range of social concerns and denominational needs. To establish such an office with a full-time professional staff person, full-time secretary, travel expenses, and program money for one particular cause constitutes a distortion of priorities and a disproportionate utilization of resources. The two people will be added to the Department of Education and Social Concern which under the department director at 25 Beacon Street currently has one staff person devoting less than full time to working on the entire range of social concerns with a part-time secretary.

I continue to support UUA efforts to eliminate discrimination and prejudice against gay people and to promote understanding and equality. First as a parish minister and then as UUA president I have initiated and encouraged such efforts. The UUA has followed a responsible course in this area of concern. Examples are the UUA sex education kit *About Your Sexuality*, the award-winning unit *The Invisible Minority*, and activities of the Department of Ministry and the administration.

The central issue in this matter is not prejudice and discrimination against gay people. The central issue is priorities among programs that serve our member congregations and address many pressing problems and needs.

As president I am subject to the direction and control of the UUA Board and, just as I developed a model for the Office, I am proceeding to establish it as voted by the Board.

I ended the editorial by urging succeeding General Assemblies to consider priorities in the whole range of Unitarian Universalist concerns. Within a few weeks, we had established the Office of

Gay Concerns and appointed Arlie Scott director. She assumed her duties in January 1975 and performed them exceptionally well. I supported her efforts and programs throughout the remainder of my tenure.

In March 1975, the *UU World* published a letter signed by 207 congregation presidents, religious education directors, and ministers, asking the UUA board to reverse its October vote and pledging support for the position set forth in the above *UU World* editorial. I reported in a subsequent interview that I stood behind my November 15 statement in its entirety but did not support a move to have the 1975 General Assembly vote to discontinue the office. My view was that "the office has just been established as a result of the General Assembly and board votes. I believe it should be given an opportunity to function."

Subsequently there were three unsuccessful efforts to terminate the office, each intended to enable the UUA to have a full-time social concerns director who would deal with a broad range of social issues, including gay concerns. One such attempt was a failed 1975 General Assembly resolution; the other two were in the form of Finance Committee recommendations to the UUA board in 1976 and 1977. In each instance, the trustees voted to continue the fully funded Office of Gay Concerns as part of UUA headquarters. The office remains a part of the UUA today. Its focus has broadened and it is now called the Office of Bisexual, Gay, Lesbian, and Transgender Concerns.

When the U.S. Supreme Court rendered its decision in April 1976 allowing states to prosecute and imprison people for committing homosexual acts, I issued a statement that termed the action a setback for all American citizens and their rights of privacy. The court ruled 6 to 3 that the right to privacy does not include the right of willing adults to engage in private sexual acts of their own chosen sexual persuasion. I said, "I agree with the dissenting judge that in the absence of harm, the government should have nothing to do with sexual activity by consenting adults in the privacy of a bedroom." I expressed my disappointment and surprise at the court's action and stated that there was "now an even heavier responsibility on state officials to preserve the basic rights of privacy for all citizens."

Committee on Aging

Though the word *office* did not appear in its title, the UUA Committee on Aging functioned in a manner similar to some of the foregoing offices associated with the UUA. In 1972, there was an active task force on aging that was a joint effort of the Women's Federation and our Association, with a UUA staff person as liaison. In October 1973, our trustees voted to establish the UUA Committee on Aging and continued to fund it every year thereafter.

The committee's activities encompassed educating, informing, and counseling congregations in areas such as awareness of federal, state, and local funds to assist the elderly; opportunities to help enact pertinent legislation; participation in the hospice movement; education for life changes; preparation for circumstances of aging parents; and new models of dignified lifestyles for older persons. There was a liaison person in each UUA district.

Our committee received acclaim and wide support from other denominations and mental health organizations for its efforts and publications. In 1975, the committee published the *Consciousness Raising* kit as phase one of a two-part series titled "Aging and Awareness." The unit was designed for intergenerational use "to enhance awareness that aging is universal, as are its processes and problems." In early 1977, the committee published the second phase entitled Advocacy. In March 1977, the UUA appointed a former executive director of the Cambridge (Massachusetts) Council on Aging to be the full-time executive secretary of the committee.

Church of the Larger Fellowship

The primary purpose of the Church of the Larger Fellowship (CLF) is to provide a ministry for isolated religious liberals, though it also offers a number of other services. When I was elected UUA president, CLF had approximately four thousand members on its rolls and was an office in our Association's headquarters organization. Its minister was a UUA employee and functioned as a UUA staff member.

In effecting the huge UUA budget reduction and reorganization in 1969, I proposed that CLF be separated from UUA headquarters and become a congregation organized like other Unitarian Universalist congregations, with its own membership, elected trustees, and fundraising operation. My recommendation included assurance that our Association would contribute space and funding as required to ensure CLF's continuing viability. The UUA board approved, and CLF was incorporated as an independent congregation in 1970. I believe its subsequent growth in strength, vitality, and services to our denomination testifies to the soundness of that decision.

Celebration and Contemplation

THE YEARS 1975 and 1976 brought two significant opportunities for celebration: the 150th anniversary of the founding of the American Unitarian Association (AUA) and the bicentennial observance of the birth of the United States of America.

UUA headquarters staff members, assisted by others in our denomination, began preparing materials in early 1974 to help congregations celebrate the birthday of the AUA. Every congregation received two packets containing program ideas and suggestions for celebrating our imminent "Year of History" in their local churches and communities, including special group activities and worship services. The mailings also enclosed items such as a capsule history of Unitarianism, a file of useful historical pictures, a reproduction of the first annual report of the AUA in 1826, and an extensive bibliography of Unitarian Universalist resource material.

The UUA Office of Information coordinated the publishing and distribution of *A Stream of Light*, a five-author history of American Unitarianism. The Association also produced and distributed other relevant material, including an anthological meditation manual and a calendar that featured historical pictures, quotations, and historical events of Unitarian Universalist significance. The Pamphlet Commission prepared a history of Unitarian pamphleteering. The UUA Department of Education and Social

Concern developed an educational curriculum on Unitarian Universalist identity, published in several parts. The first emphasized the relevance of our denomination's history to the current reality. In January 1975, all congregations received their third packet of materials.

May 25, 1825, was the precise date the AUA was founded. Our UUA Public Relations Office prepared a three-minute tape of a message from me for use in a variety of television settings, including programs commemorating the sesquicentennial anniversary. In the tape, produced specifically for a Philadelphia television station for broadcast in May, I discussed the special relationship of Unitarian Universalist religion to contemporary society. The UUA also made available to congregations an audiocassette tape and illustrated booklet for use on May 25; one side of the tape consisted of an interview with Conrad Wright, professor of American church history at Harvard Divinity School and editor of *A Stream of Light*, who described and commented on the founding of the AUA. The other side conveyed greetings from Bishop Kovacs of the Transylvanian-Romanian Unitarian churches; Bishop Ferencz of the Hungarian Unitarian churches on behalf of their president Bela Bartok; and Brian Golland, general secretary of the Unitarian churches in Great Britain and Ireland—all were the institutional predecessors of Unitarian churches in America.

On Sunday, May 25, 1975, Unitarian Universalists throughout the continent marked the founding of the American Unitarian Association in Boston exactly 150 years earlier. In many locales, our congregations met in clusters for common services and celebrations. That afternoon, UUA moderator Joseph Fisher and I participated in a special service and wreath laying at the Jefferson Memorial in Washington that was attended by numerous members from area congregations. A few days later, several hundred Unitarian Universalists were in Boston's Symphony Hall for "Unitarian Night at the Pops," a musical tribute by the Boston Pops Orchestra. Soon afterward, a huge birthday party and banquet was the concluding event at the 1975 General Assembly in Minneapolis.

Among the many talks and addresses I gave during the anniversary year, one I especially remember was a sermon in the First Unitarian Church of Cincinnati during the joint service of Unitarian Universalist congregations in the greater Cincinnati area, celebrating both the AUA anniversary and the birthday of William Howard Taft. The only person in history to hold the positions of president of the United States and chief justice of the Supreme Court, Taft was an enthusiastic and active Unitarian from his youth in the Cincinnati church until the day he died. As "statesman and jurist, he served his nation in many capacities," I noted,

> Though a less remembered achievement, his diplomatic missions earned him the unofficial title of "Secretary of Peace" in the press of such nations as Russia, China, and Japan. He was a foremost advocate of world peace and the means for organizing the achievement of it. He was a strong supporter of the League of Nations and spoke throughout the country in its behalf. . . . All through his life he made his Unitarian identification clear. He never backed down from his Unitarian beliefs, though often he was baited as an atheist and agnostic. He demonstrated until the very end a deep devotion to the work of our denomination.

Taft held numerous offices in a variety of Unitarian organizations and endeavors, including six years as vice president of the American Unitarian Association. Though a lifelong member of the Cincinnati congregation, he also joined All Souls Unitarian Church in Washington, where he presided at the annual parish meeting, addressed a series of Sunday evening meetings, laid the cornerstone for the church's present building on Sixteenth Street, and spoke at its dedication. While chief justice of the Supreme Court, he took time to visit the church school and talk with children.

I also mentioned that not much was said of Taft's Unitarianism until the days of the presidential campaign, when his unorthodox religious views were bitterly though subtly attacked in a whispering campaign.

In a speech at First Church in Boston, Taft told New England
Unitarians that they did not understand the attitude of people in
other parts of the country toward Unitarianism. He said, "If you
want to find out run for President."

President Theodore Roosevelt once said of Taft that it was one
of his great gifts that he possessed the ability unflinchingly to
stand by the right, and yet do it with the minimum of offensive-
ness toward those who did not see matters as he did. He was
known for his kindness, fairness, and intelligence . . . and was profoundly interested to the last in the strengthening and extension of
our free faith.

Bicentennial

Our denominational planning for celebrating the U.S. bicentennial began in 1974. A large portion of our preparation was
grounded in a joint effort coordinated by the National Council of
Churches (NCC): Project FORWARD 76, an acronym for "freedom of religion will advance real democracy." The project originated when a number of church leaders of various faiths became
concerned about the approaching bicentennial, specifically, that
some aspects of religious freedom might be overlooked in the celebration. A former executive secretary of the council was engaged
full time to head the endeavor.

FORWARD 76, staffed by the NCC interfaith center in New
York, was an interfaith national organization expressly created to
convey the importance of religious freedom in bicentennial celebrations. I was one of the organizers and served on the continuing
policy committee, which met regularly to give guidance to the staff
on matters of content and direction. The project enjoyed a wide
group of sponsors: In mid-1974 I commented to the UUA board
upon the singularity of people with such diverse religious views
joining together on an issue.

The UUA created a program designed primarily to aid local
congregations in observing the bicentennial. It emphasized four

key elements: religious freedom as a basic source of other freedoms, Unitarian Universalist history and values as they relate to the founding of the United States, assessment of the present and future concerning "unfinished business" of the nation, and the dangers of civil religion and religious materialism. UUA headquarters staff developed and distributed resource materials, and made FORWARD 76 publications available to our churches and fellowships. The Association trustees appointed a Committee of Correspondence to implement our bicentennial program and particularly to enhance participation, communication, and sharing among congregations. Each member of the committee was responsible for the geographic area in which he or she lived, with staff support from the UUA departments of Education and Social Concern, Publications, and Ministry.

In the fall of 1974, I sent a letter about the bicentennial to ministers and leaders of all Unitarian Universalist congregations. I enclosed two copies of "So You Want to Observe the Bicentennial . . . Project FORWARD 76 Wants to Help" and urged each congregation to schedule a special date for a bicentennial observance on a common Sunday in the spring of 1976. I also mentioned that FORWARD 76 had produced an incredibly rich resource book titled *Religious Freedom in America*, with an accompanying study outline by three distinguished scholars. In closing I wrote, "We must not leave the bicentennial celebration to the merchandisers, marchers, and religious nationalism. We have a critical role. I trust that you will join with me in fulfilling it."

Early the next year, the Committee of Correspondence announced it had adopted as a bicentennial theme "The Real American Revolution Continues" and suggested the first Sunday in May 1976 as a common date for special bicentennial observances. In May that year, UUA executive vice president Robert Senghas and publications director Doris Pullen joined me in representing our Association at a two-day "Consultation on Religion and the Bicentennial" in Washington, which was co-sponsored by Project FORWARD 76 and the American Revolution Bicentennial Administration. A clearinghouse for exchanging information was established at UUA headquarters, and by fall 1975 the committee had sent resource packets to congregations.

In July 1975, I was one of nine leaders of American religious bodies invited to meet with President Gerald Ford at the White House to present a special bicentennial collection of American prayer proclamations. Two hundred years earlier, the Second Continental Congress had issued the first such national proclamation, signed by John Hancock, who was president of the congress and an active Unitarian layman. That original proclamation asked all Americans to observe a day of prayer addressed to the "Great Governor of the World" to preserve their new union and secure civil and religious liberties.

In the intervening two centuries, there were 182 similar proclamations by presidents and congresses. Our group presented bound vellum facsimiles of all of them to President Ford. Two presidents who issued proclamations for a national day of prayer and thanksgiving were Unitarians: John Adams and William Howard Taft.

I was one of four hundred invited participants who attended the Bicentennial Conference on Religious Liberty in Philadelphia in April 1976. The participants included scholars, clergy, lawyers, educators, civil rights activists, historians, and community leaders. Outstanding scholars addressed the conference on a range of topics concerned with religious liberty in the United States.

Though most bicentennial activities focused on 1976, there were numerous related events the preceding year, notably those associated with the battles of Lexington and Concord that occurred in April 1775 and marked the beginning of the Revolutionary War. Thus April 19, 1975, was the formal beginning for many observances and celebrations of the nation's two-hundredth birthday. In March of that year at a meeting of Unitarian Universalists gathered in Denver, I spoke about the events of 1775 and 1776 and their relationship to contemporary society. Though military battles certainly were essential, I emphasized that there was far more to the Revolution:

We are in danger as a nation if our observance of the bicentennial degenerates into a reenacting of battles and a glorying in our military triumphs. . . . For too many Americans it has already become a huckster's heaven and a superpatriot's dream. . . .

We do grave disservice to our Unitarian Universalist principles if we abandon the bicentennial observances to those who would promote the worst of our nationalism or simply make a fast buck. The issues inherent in the founding of our nation are still with us. The real American Revolution continues, for the real American Revolution was not a series of battles or fighting speeches.

I recalled the observation of historian Samuel Eliot Morison concerning the opening words in the Declaration of Independence about equality and the inalienable rights of life, liberty, and the pursuit of happiness. He described those words as "more revolutionary than anything written by Robespierre, Marx, or Lenin; more explosive than the atom, a continual challenge to ourselves, as well as to the oppressed of the world."

Discussing some specific current issues involving those declared rights and Unitarian Universalist ideals, I began by saying that the rights to life, liberty and the pursuit of happiness certainly include quality of life:

Some in our time take the phrase "right to life" and pervert its meaning. Our concern ought always to be not *that* we live but *how* we live. Two of the most controversial concerns of our time deal with just this question of the right to the quality of life.

I named the two issues as abortion and the environment, and I went on to discuss those and several other contemporary issues linked to the words of the Declaration, among them governmental abuse of power, censorship, and school desegregation:

Members of our Unitarian Universalist congregations have

today the opportunity—I would say the obligation—to work to ensure that the bicentennial is as much a recognition of the current issues as it is in honor of our past achievements. Principles basic to our Unitarian Universalist religion underlie the founding of this nation . . .

Our American ideals are not simply a legacy given to us by our ancestors. They are the kind of inheritance that becomes ours only as we earn them in our time, only as we defend and protect them with as much vigor as did those who went before us. . . . In our time—in Colorado as well as Concord, in Cheyenne as well as Virginia—we give our efforts to continuing the real American Revolution, to completing the uncompleted agenda.

View After Six Years

The AUA anniversary and U.S. bicentennial were occasions for contemplating where we had been as a religious movement, our present values, and where we were headed. In November 1975, during the annual meeting of the Tennessee Unitarian Universalist Conference, I gave an address entitled "What Are We? A View of Our Denomination After Six Years As President." That evening, I shared some of my thoughts about our denomination based on my experience during the past six years. Having just commemorated the beginning of our organized religious movement in America, it seemed appropriate to examine what we found ourselves to be three-quarters of the way through the twentieth century.

In my talk, I concluded a review of some present-day aspects by discussing cooperation, citing the recent comments of some observers that what was needed in the United States was the reestablishment of a sense that beneath the turbulent surface of national life was a basic mutuality of interests, a set of commonly accepted values. "I believe that is what is needed in our denomination today. We must grow up from the 'I' to the 'We': We are lost as a nation, we are lost as a world, and we are lost as a denomination if we do not have the maturity to grow up from the 'I' to the 'We.' Individualism, as much as we cherish it, can be misapplied and taken to extremes." My message that evening was that we are all in this together. There is not another liberal religious denomination of comparable size on this continent. We were needed then, we are needed now, and we will be needed in the future.

I urged a sense of openness as we moved toward the future—openness toward the searching of so many in our culture—and I particularly stressed the need to concentrate on the central tasks of all our congregations, meaning and community.

The remainder of my address was devoted to some recent trends and a few comments concerning my attitude toward the future. I noted that we were nearing the end of a period of anti-institutionalism, both in our own denomination and in the culture at large. There was more participation in our congregations and an increased awareness of the need for community in a liberal religious congregation.

I observed that things were going reasonably well for our denomination. Our membership figures had dropped less than a half percent that year, which was better than in the mainstream denominations. The financial contributions to our congregations were continuing to grow: $3 million above the previous year, an increase of more than 12 percent. For the first time in a number of years, congregations gave $29 thousand more to the UUA than they did the year before and thus reversed a trend. There was more warmth evident in our congregations and programs; heightened concern for enriching worship and common celebration; greater interest in theology; and renewed, widespread interest in extension. I perceived those as signs of health.

In spite of problems, I was optimistic: "For I am aware of what this religious movement has meant in the lives of people and communities, and I believe that will continue." I was convinced we would do better. We had a responsibility to do better:

When it comes right down to it, I am aware that it will be the people that count, and I believe we have the people who do not mind working against adversity, who cherish the principle of the free mind, who are dedicated to a free worship, who want to build not just for their own good but for others, who are soundly grounded in their own religious approach. Basically I am optimistic because of a self-correcting quality in our approach to church polity and religion, a balancing quality. And because I know we have people who are devoted to the free religious ideal—for which there is a need and will continue to be a need.

We as a denomination will continue going through change, for we are in a changing culture and society continentally, just as many of us individually live in changing neighborhoods and cities. There always will be an institution of liberal religion. The question is its form. If we can hold meaning and community paramount—if they are at the core, the grounding from which we act—we will move closer to fulfilling our potential. The future is in the hands of those who care for the institution.

What I would say to you is: Mold that institution, shape it, and change it, but do not destroy it—because you need it and people out there need it, and people in the future are going to need it. We talk about the use of reason and intelligence: Use them. We talk about change: Be willing to accept it. We talk about caring: Do it. And not just in one's inner circle. Let us keep our eyes open and do some thinking and make those words become a reality.

I still believe today that the touchstone of our religious community is freedom with responsibility. Victor Frankl, the renowned psychotherapist, said our greatest freedom is the freedom to choose how we respond to our circumstances. I'm optimistic because of the courage and conscience bequeathed to us by our heritage—a courage and conscience we will bring to bear in our own as well as the larger community.

Unitarian Universalist Advance

Midway through my second term, a group of ministerial and lay leaders formed Unitarian Universalist Advance as a vehicle for encouraging the UUA board, officers, and members "in the advancement of the Association's purpose as stated in its bylaws." Its objectives were to bring more focus to our denomination's religious life and to promote the advance of the Unitarian Universalist faith in thought and action. During the 1975 UUA General Assembly, a group of 216 people took steps to form a permanent organization.

Three months later, Advance leaders announced seven study groups. Within a year, the organization produced more than a dozen study papers and conducted a two-day session in Madison, Wisconsin, which included discussion of the attributes needed in the next UUA president. That event was followed by a November 1976 theological conference in Chicago, a February 1977 conference in Florida on "the Unitarian Universalist mission," and an April 1977 conference in San Francisco on social action.

Eliminating President and Moderator

In October 1975, a board retreat produced three proposals to change the roles and functions of our denomination's two top officers: to eliminate the positions of president and moderator by having the board appoint the UUA chief executive officer, not to be called president; the board elect its own chairperson; and the General Assembly elect an officer, not to be called moderator, to be the ceremonial and spiritual spokesperson for the Association. During the subsequent board meeting and discussion, moderator Joseph Fisher stated that the proposed changes would put an enormous amount of power in the hands of the board. He cautioned the trustees to proceed slowly, adding that "this will be seen by many as a grab for power by the board."

Nevertheless, the core of the board's recommendations appeared on the business agenda of the 1976 General Assembly in the form of proposed amendments to the UUA bylaws, worded so as not to affect the current moderator and president. Shortly before the assembly convened, the board voted to oppose its own recommendation that the office of president be eliminated, yet support its proposal that the trustees appoint the board chairperson in lieu of the UUA moderator performing that function. The General Assembly did not approve the proposed bylaw changes.

Our Religious Values

Throughout my adult lifetime, our religion has usually been described as a noncreedal, nonauthoritarian approach defined by four core characteristics:

- individual freedom to arrive at religious truth as we perceive it, and to change our beliefs in light of new knowledge and experience
- the use of reason in arriving at religious beliefs
- respect for the right of other persons to hold and express differing religious beliefs
- responsibility to apply one's religious beliefs in daily living

In 1976, Dr. Robert Miller of Tufts University published a study that defined us from a different perspective. His theory was that Unitarian Universalists were not less religious than members of other denominations but *differently* religious. He had two thousand members of our congregations, a carefully selected representative sample, rank two sets of eighteen values. He then measured their ranking against the results of a famous study done five years earlier involving Catholics, Protestants, Jews, and people with no religious affiliation.

Dr. Miller's study found that we indeed differ significantly in our value patterns from other Protestants, Catholics, Jews, and people with no religious affiliation. For example, in order of highest ranking, the top seven values ranked by Unitarian Universalists on the first set of eighteen were self-respect, wisdom, freedom, family security, inner harmony, a sense of accomplishment, and mature love. At the bottom of our list was salvation, a word commonly used to measure whether a person is religious or not. From the second set of values the highest six for our members were honest, broadminded, loving, responsible, courageous, and independent—at the bottom of our list was obedient.

The study demonstrated that there is a distinctive Unitarian Universalist pattern of religiousness. One of Dr. Miller's findings was that we are a strongly homogeneous group when it comes to our religious values. Another was that our value system is clearly distinguishable from other religious bodies as well as from people claiming no religious affiliation. He found that we have a value system characterized by inner direction, personal realization, self-fulfillment, and self-actualization—an internalization of the ethical norm rather than being told we must achieve something that is labeled a value. It means we place emphasis on engaging in a process to try to achieve our ideals and practice our religion.

The Miller study supported and expanded on the findings of our denomination's "Goals Study" ten years earlier: that being religious for us involves searching for meaning in our personal and social lives, pondering our place in the ultimate scheme of things, trying to handle our joys and our tragedies, seeking profound and satisfying human relationships, and being aware of the difference between our potential and our achievements.

Public Relations and Social Action

BASED ON HIS 1976 study of our denomination, Dr. Robert Miller observed that Unitarian Universalists place emphasis on engaging in a process "to try to achieve our ideals and practice our religion." His observation is relevant not only to daily personal decisions and interactions but also to social actions and public issues such as the Vietnam War, abortion rights, the death penalty, racial injustice, and civil liberties.

In conjunction with that emphasis, I encouraged promoting the broadest possible understanding of what we are and what we do. During my tenure, I strongly advocated devoting more attention and money to public relations and the electronic media, especially television, but in response to General Assembly votes the board continually allocated funds for other purposes. In the 1970–1971 UUA budget, for example, our total annual amount for public relations was cut to $1 thousand. The first significant amount for publicity came from the block grants that the Veatch program began funding in mid-1974 (see the chapter "The Veatch Program and Holdeen Trusts").

When I filed the required petitions in January 1973 to run for a second term, I named public awareness as my first priority. I said we must "attempt to create greater public awareness of our Unitarian Universalist religion and movement, greater public awareness of what we are and what we are doing" and urged a major emphasis on television and radio: "Historically we have used the written word effectively. Today we also must utilize electronic media to communicate Unitarian Universalist ideals and values."

In January 1975, we broadened the services of the UUA Public Relations Office by engaging a full-time director who had experience with television. Besides working on projects such as our 150th anniversary celebration, the director conducted public relations workshops for Unitarian Universalist conferences, district meetings, clusters, and some individual congregations. *UU Media News*, a resource of denominational and media-related information; new advertising materials; books and materials on promotion, publicity, and public relations; television and radio spots; and a special part of the Sharing In Growth program (see the chapter "Identity and Sharing In Growth Programs") were developed and offered. The director also produced three television spots about child abuse, which were offered to television stations as a public service and broadcast in a number of localities across the continent.

The trustees approved my proposal for denominational coordination of funding for television, radio, and audiovisual projects in October 1976. Among other provisions, the tentative arrangement called for a seven-member committee that would administer funds given to our Association by the Veatch program for that specific purpose and finance a Unitarian Universalist television-radio-audiovisual center, which would not have production facilities. The proposal required approval and funding by the Veatch program in order to be implemented. At the time I left office in June 1977, no agreement had been reached with the Veatch program regarding the plan, and the UUA board had appointed a media planning committee to pursue the matter.

Vietnam War

The Vietnam War was highly controversial in our congregations and in our denomination at large, particularly in the earlier part of the 1960s. I believe it was the primary cause of the anti-institutionalism and confrontational politics that were pervasive in much of American society and rampant in our denomination at the time of my election. The war certainly was the most divisive issue in our religious movement until the black-empowerment controversy arose in 1968 (see the chapter "BUUC and BAC").

Many Unitarian Universalists were active in antiwar endeavors, and a sizeable number were elected as antiwar delegates to the 1968 Democratic National Convention. Despite widespread differences of opinion, UUA General Assemblies approved resolutions that questioned—and later opposed—U.S. involvement in the conflict. In time, the anti-Vietnam War sentiment within our denomination intensified and broadened.

A few weeks after I entered office in the summer of 1969, a huge antiwar rally took place on Boston Common across the street from UUA headquarters. To make the viewpoint of our Association known, I arranged to place a four-story net with large letters on the front of our building; the letters spelled out an excerpt from the most recent General Assembly resolution about the war. The *UU World* newspaper, which began publication in March 1970, reflected numerous and sustained efforts by Unitarian Universalists to end the Vietnam War, often in concert with other denominations. News reports, letters to the editor, editorials, and photographs conveyed the antiwar sentiments, demonstrations, and other activities of individuals and congregations as well as the UUA administration, board, and General Assemblies.

On December 22, 1972, I sent a telegram to President Nixon about the decision to resume bombing North Vietnam four days earlier:

> Christmas decorations and festivities at the White House are an abomination and blatant hypocrisy as our killing in Vietnam continues. Your latest bombing actions are killing the moral sensitivity in our American spirit. In the name of the best in your religion, as well as the best in our American tradition, stop our participation in the war.

A month later, I spoke at a two-hour service at the National United Methodist Church on Inauguration Sunday. It was the closing event of the "Inauguration of Conscience" held in Washington concurrent with the presidential inauguration, which brought together an estimated 100 thousand people in affirmation and renewal of their commitment to make peace a reality. I mentioned that, in contemplating my own thoughts and feelings during the recent days of B-52 slaughter in Vietnam, I found particularly apt two sentences from a letter written by a European friend, a man who had been a staunch supporter of the United States:

> I might say quite truly that your bombers, while devastating North Vietnam, were also shattering your image, destroying the high moral reputation that through so many years you had so well deserved by unprecedented acts of good will. But however important the image you offer to others, infinitely more important is your conscience; and what I might say to my many friends is quite simply: "This is not like you, and if you tolerate this you are betraying your character."

I went on to say,

> We are told our participation in the war will end soon—let us hope it is true. But in these days when so much is being said about what message the president received from the American people, let us make certain he now hears: *This must not happen again!*
>
> And we should be aware of another casualty of this war—American freedom: Here at home, our freedom, basic liberties are ignored or trampled underfoot by our current government, specifically freedom of the press, privacy, freedom of religion, academic freedom. . . . Recently we have witnessed reporters and a university professor jailed; unusual government pressure on television and newspapers; use of grand juries to intimidate and harass and to repress legitimate dissent; military and political surveillance; and other disturbing instances of government incursions upon individual liberty.

So let this time be for us not only an inauguration of conscience, but also an inauguration of concern for freedom —American freedom—here at home, yours and mine, and all other citizens' in this land, which is still a democracy, not a seventeenth-century monarchy.

U.S. combat troops withdrew from Vietnam in late March 1973, and our bombing of Cambodia ceased that August. Commenting on the ending of the war, Secretary of State Henry Kissinger said, "Now we must make peace with ourselves." In September 1974, the UUA Department of Education and Social Concern launched a campaign to encourage Congress to expand President Ford's recently announced clemency program into an unconditional, universal amnesty for war resisters. The effort entailed contacting congressional officials and soliciting our congregations' active support.

The war finally ended in April 1975 with the fall of Saigon and abandonment of the U.S. embassy. On the day our marines departed the embassy, I gave a brief address expressing thanksgiving that the "bloodshed and killing and human destruction is at an end." I continued,

Many of us have been working for a number of years trying to point out the futility and destructiveness of the course our government leaders of both parties were pursuing. I think back and remember that the General Assembly of our denomination has passed statements about Vietnam every year since 1964—and Beacon Press, our denomination's publishing house, published the full version of the Pentagon Papers when they were made public. I believe that at times our efforts and those of others opposed to the war were misunderstood. Many of our government leaders seemed unable to recognize honest dissent based upon religious and ethical convictions and genuine concern for our nation.

I hope we—the citizens and leaders of our nation—have learned a lesson, and that lesson will save future bloodshed and misery. We cannot solve everybody's problems in the world. We cannot impose our way upon everyone. I hope we realize that the war not only tore at Vietnam and its people, but at our own nation: our government, our economy, our life. Much that we now suffer from inflation and unemployment, for example, is attributable to our being in the Vietnam War, and the terrible thing is we did not have to be in it.

I believe we in our country should not engage in a period of trying to fix blame, but we should move on to trying to build our nation so it is stronger economically and in the practice of democracy. I believe pain and error can be great contributors to wisdom and maturity. I hope our nation is wiser and more mature.

In December 1976, I joined U.S. Senator Edward Brooke at UUA headquarters for a press conference in which we urged support of a national petition campaign calling on President Ford to declare unconditional amnesty for Vietnam War resisters. I opened the occasion by commenting on the appropriateness of it being held at UUA headquarters because our Association supported general amnesty and because Gold Star Parents for Amnesty operated from our headquarters building. ("Gold Star parents" are parents of members of the armed services who die during a period of war.) As part of the press conference, a local representative of the American Friends Service Committee presented petitions bearing 13 thousand signatures to Senator Brooke, who said unconditional amnesty was the only way to "heal the wounds of the Vietnam War." The title of the petition drive was "Lest We Forget: An Appeal for Reconciliation."

Impeachment

Richard Nixon was elected president in 1968 and ran again in 1972 with overwhelming success. In September 1971, the "White House Plumbers" burglarized a psychiatrist's office seeking files about Daniel Ellsberg, who had leaked the Pentagon Papers (see the chapter "Pentagon Papers"). In June 1972, five men were arrested at the Watergate complex in Washington while attempting to bug Democratic National Committee headquarters; the FBI subsequently determined that their mission was part of a massive campaign of political spying and sabotage conducted on behalf of the Nixon reelection effort. In January 1973, the five Watergate intruders and two of Nixon's aides were found guilty of conspiracy, burglary, and wiretapping. In late April, the president announced the forced departure of his top two aides, as well as the attorney general and White House counsel, because of their involvement in the scandal.

In May 1973, the Senate Watergate Committee began its nationally televised hearings, a special prosecutor was appointed, the former White House counsel told investigators he had discussed the Watergate cover-up with Nixon at least thirty-five times, and prosecutors found a White House memo describing in detail the plans to burglarize the office of Ellsberg's psychiatrist. Congressional and newspaper investigations revealed evidence of a conspiracy to cover up a widespread operation aimed at sabotaging the president's political rivals to assure his reelection. In July, defying a federal court order, Nixon refused to turn over presidential tape recordings to the Senate committee or the special prosecutor. On the night of October 19, Nixon fired the special Watergate prosecutor, abolished the office, and impounded its records; the new attorney general and deputy attorney general resigned in protest.

Five days later, the UUA trustees passed a resolution stating that the "best way to resolve this crisis is for the House of Representatives to institute formal impeachment proceedings." The board also authorized me to make available to the House Judiciary Committee all information regarding the harassment of our denomination in the Beacon Press-Pentagon Papers matter.

In a front-page November 1 *UU World* editorial, I stated, "Until the events of October 19–20, I was among those opposed to initiating impeachment proceedings. Now I believe the American people have no choice other than impeaching the President." I asked if we really believe what we teach our children in civics books, and continued, "No less is at stake than the soul of the American people."

I joined eighteen national religious leaders in March 1974 to announce formation of the Religious Committee for Integrity in Government, a nonpartisan, interfaith committee of Washington-based denominational staff members. The committee was charged to work toward clarification of critical moral issues in the current crisis; justice for the president and the American people, through an orderly and expeditious inquiry by the House Judiciary Committee into grounds for impeachment; campaign reform, including public financing of campaigns; restoration of constitutional checks and balances in the federal government through congressional vigilance toward its own constitutional responsibilities; and clarification of critical moral issues facing the electorate in 1974 and 1976.

On July 24, the Supreme Court ruled unanimously that Nixon must turn over tape recordings of sixty-four White House conversations. Three days later, the House Judiciary Committee passed the first of three articles of impeachment, charging obstruction of justice. On August 9, 1974, Richard Nixon became the first U.S. president to resign from office.

The new president was Gerald Ford, who precisely one month later granted a "full, free, and absolute pardon" to Nixon for all offenses he might have committed from January 1969 to August 1974. The new special prosecutor had been working on ten areas of possible action against Nixon, including harassment of enemies. In granting the pardon, Ford said,

> I have promised to uphold the Constitution to do what is right as God gives me to see the right. . . . Only the laws of God, which govern our consciences, are superior to it. As we are a nation under God, so I am sworn to uphold our laws with the help of God. And I have sought such guidance and searched my own conscience. . . .

Two days later, I sent a telegram to President Ford:

Though I am one who does not wish Richard Nixon to go to jail, I must express my strong objection to the nature and timing of the pardon. Your action subverts the judicial institutions of our nation, undermines confidence in our American political process, and weakens your credibility. Please stop blaming God in your speeches for the actions of Gerald Ford.

I also wrote a letter to the *New York Times* the same day. That paper did not publish my letter, but the *UU World* did on October 1:

Among the troubling aspects of President Ford's pardon was the attempt in his opening statement to place responsibility on God. Despite Ford's declaration that the buck stopped with him, he tried to pass it up higher.

The God that sustains President Ford is the same God that sustains everyone. Numerous citizens, Republicans and Democrats, persons for and against pardon, search their consciences deeply when trying to decide what is right. Gerald Ford has no special pipeline to God.

The President will better serve our nation if he resists the temptation to equate his decisions with those of deity. When he speaks it is the voice of Ford, not the voice of the Lord.

Abortion Rights

Unitarian Universalist laity, clergy, and denominational leaders have long supported and worked for the right of every woman to have access to safe, legal abortions and to freely make her own decision regarding whether to continue her pregnancy. The 1963 and 1968 UUA general assemblies passed resolutions on abortion rights, the 1968 statement urging that "efforts be made to abolish existing abortion laws except to prohibit performance of an abortion by a person who is not a duly licensed physician, leaving the decision as to an abortion to the doctor and his patient."

At the January 1971 board meeting, I reported my recent involvement in the controversy concerning Massachusetts abortion laws and indicated that my name would appear on a bill in the legislature to repeal the current restrictive statute. A few weeks later, I testified before the Massachusetts legislature about the proposed change in abortion legislation. In May 1972, the UUA trustees voted to lend $100 thousand to Preterm, a pregnancy counseling service, for the purpose of purchasing a building; UUA designated funds enabled us to make the two-year loan, and the Preterm real estate provided security.

In January 1973, the U.S. Supreme Court announced its *Roe v. Wade* decision, which held that a woman's right to an abortion fell within the right to privacy protected by the Constitution. The ruling gave women the right to abortion during the entirety of a pregnancy, yet defined different levels of states' interest in regulating abortion during the second and third trimesters.

The struggle concerning abortion rights continued at the state level despite that decision. Legislatures passed laws against abortion, and a campaign was launched to amend the federal Constitution. In April, the *UU World* reported that the Supreme Court decision wasn't working in most states: Hospitals and doctors were not cooperating and district attorneys were ignoring the *Roe v. Wade* ruling. Many Unitarian Universalists actively supported pro-choice efforts during that critical period, working to achieve the goal of having high-quality, low-cost abortions available to women in every state. The UUA and Women's Federation joined others in filing amicus briefs before the U.S. Supreme Court on behalf of Texas and Georgia appellants, who were ultimately successful. The 1973 General Assembly passed a resolution stating that whereas "there are well-organized efforts of letter writing, petitions, and a Washington office for lobbying to amend the Constitution to overturn the Supreme Court decision on abortion; be it resolved that we support the Supreme Court ruling on abortion and its implementation."

In February 1975, Dr. Kenneth Edelin, the first black physician in the history of Boston City Hospital to be appointed chief resident of obstetrics/gynecology, was convicted of manslaughter for the alleged death of a fetus following a legal abortion. His patient, a seventeen-year-old unmarried woman who had been brought to him by her mother for an abortion, had a normal recovery. However, a series of actions by Boston politicians—including a state legislator, city councilman, and county district attorney— culminated in a six-week trial and guilty verdict. The UUA, with seven other religious groups, joined the *Edelin* case as friends of the court in an appeal to the Massachusetts Supreme Judicial Court, which overturned the doctor's conviction.

The 1975 General Assembly passed a resolution stating that it reaffirmed "the right of any female of any age or marital or economical status to have an abortion at her own request upon medical/social consultation of her own choosing" and urged Unitarian Universalists to "resist through their elected representatives the efforts now underway by some members of the Congress of the United States and state legislatures to curtail that right by means of constitutional amendment or other means."

In January 1976, on the eve of the third anniversary of the *Roe v. Wade* decision, I joined six national religious leaders in Washington for a press conference called by the Religious Coalition for Abortion Rights, which represented twenty-three religious groups. The other participants were from the United Methodist Church, United Church of Christ, Union of American Hebrew Congregations, National Council of Jewish Women, American Baptist Churches, and United Presbyterian Church. Commenting on the proposed constitutional amendment to outlaw abortion, I stated that religious freedom was at issue:

> The fire that fuels the abortion controversy is religious belief, the attempt to impose on everyone a particular religious belief. The Supreme Court has said that cannot be done in our land.
>
> Religious freedom as protected by the First Amendment is precious. The proposed amendment to outlaw abortion is

a direct attack on that freedom of belief protected by the First Amendment; it would in effect amend the First Amendment. Certainly people are free to hold and to practice differing beliefs regarding abortion. The 1973 Supreme Court decision imposes no such belief or practice upon anyone, but permits freedom of choice, freedom to follow one's own conscience, freedom to practice one's own faith. And that is as it should be. The question of abortion should be left to each individual to decide according to one's own belief and conscience.

The UUA, Women's Federation, and eleven other major religious organizations formed the Massachusetts Coalition for Abortion Rights in early 1976. In September, two days before the election debate by presidential candidates Gerald Ford and Jimmy Carter, I spoke in Philadelphia at a press conference called by the National Coalition for Abortion Rights to protest the manner in which the abortion issue had been raised in the presidential campaign. Among the other panelists were a Methodist bishop, a Reform rabbi, and representatives from the United Presbyterian Church and United Church of Christ. Portions of our statements received national television coverage on evening news programs.

I also wrote separate letters to presidential candidates Ford and Carter in which I termed the proposed constitutional amendments on abortion a "direct attack on religious liberty" and noted that the thrust of the recent Supreme Court decision was that "a decision regarding abortion should be determined by one's own conscience and not by the dictates of government." Declaring that "the proposed Constitutional amendments are an attempt to impose on everyone a particular religious practice," I urged Ford to de-escalate the abortion issue and Carter to hold firm against pressure for antiabortion amendments to the Constitution. I specifically called on Ford to "reconsider (1) elevating the abortion controversy as a major issue in the election campaign, and (2) your reported position favoring a constitutional amendment placing the matter of antiabortion legislation in the hands of state governments." I also urged Ford to "distinguish your personal views from your official responsibility as president." My particular plea to Carter was that he "avoid complicity in a so-called compromise arrangement that would punish the poor by denying government funds for medical aid connected with abortion."

In early October, the UUA and Women's Federation joined nine other religious organizations as friends of the court in litigation to prevent cutting off federal Medicaid funds to women who have abortions. Our brief, filed in federal court in Brooklyn, New York, declared that legislation such as the recently instituted Hyde amendment was based on a single religious doctrine and thus violated the First Amendment's constitutional guarantees against the government's establishment of religion. The Hyde amendment provided that no funds of the Department of Health, Education, and Welfare—including Medicaid funds—could be used for abortion except where a woman's life was endangered. On October 22, 1976, the court issued an order prohibiting the federal government from implementing the Hyde amendment. The ruling applied in all fifty states and made it unconstitutional for the government to deny funds for abortion to Medicaid patients.

Death Penalty

In 1961, the delegates at our first General Assembly passed a resolution urging congregations "to exert all reasonable efforts toward the elimination of capital punishment." The 1966 General Assembly passed a similar resolution calling for "the complete abolition of capital punishment in all United States and Canadian jurisdictions."

In a 1972 Georgia case, the U.S. Supreme Court ruled that the death penalty was unconstitutional. Justice William J. Brennan Jr., in his concurring opinion, held it to be unconstitutional under the Eighth Amendment, which prohibits "cruel and unusual punishments." Consequently most people believed capital punishment in the United States had ended, but some dissenting justices in the case left the door open to reinstating the death penalty if it were applied equally to all citizens. Sure enough, the Supreme Court held in a July 1976 decision that the Georgia legislature had taken steps to have the death penalty equitably administered to a convicted felon named Troy Gregg, which meant all states could reinstitute the death penalty. Three weeks later, the UUA joined a number of other national organizations that were committed to abolishing capital punishment in forming the National Coalition Against the Death Penalty. We realized that the Gregg decision raised the possibility of a large number of people being executed within a short time.

Troy Gregg died in a prison-break shooting before the state of Georgia could execute him. In Utah, however, inmate Gary Gilmore requested that his death sentence be carried out. I sent a telegram to the Utah Board of Pardons saying that the UUA urged a permanent stay of execution for Gilmore and that "the moral principle against capital punishment should override Gilmore's wish to use the state of Utah to accomplish his own death." If the sentence were carried out, Gilmore would be the first person executed since the Supreme Court reinstated the death penalty.

The Utah board did not block the execution. On January 16, 1977, I joined sixteen religious leaders from nine other denominations for an all-night vigil outside the prison walls in Utah prior to Gilmore's death. Members of our group took turns throughout the night maintaining the vigil. During my segment, we received word that a stay had been issued. However, during our 7:15 A.M. worship service, we learned that the execution would proceed, as attorneys for the state of Utah had flown to Denver during the night and persuaded a panel of judges to overrule the stay. All of us promptly returned to the prison walls and remained silent until after the execution; I held a large placard bearing the hand-lettered words "Why do we kill people who kill people to show that killing is wrong?"

In a subsequent statement, I said it was tragic that "our nation has headed back down the road to killing people. We are one of the few countries in the western hemisphere to practice capital punishment. When the government kills a person each of us is involved—all of us citizens are responsible. There is no established evidence that capital punishment is a deterrent to crime. Those of us who believe in the sacredness of life and living a civilized existence will have to use what influence we have to stop capital punishment in this country."

Center City Church Conference

In October 1972, the UUA Department of Education and Social Concern sponsored a four-day "Center City Church Conference" in Philadelphia to probe problems and challenges of churches in larger cities. Hundreds of hours of work by planning committee members and attendees preceded the event. The conference planners sent eight-page profile questionnaires to approximately 120 congregations in cities with populations of more than fifty thousand and encouraged each participating church to send a team of at least five members. Some two hundred persons attended from forty-three churches, situated in twenty-nine cities in the eastern and central United States and three Canadian provinces. During the four days, participants heard professionals from various fields speak and engaged in twenty workshops, seeking answers to center city church and society problems.

There were follow-up activities in different cities and regions during subsequent years. A national "center city church" organization formed in 1974 with ten congregations as initial members. Churches joining were entitled to free consultation concerning center city issues.

Corporate Practices

In 1971, there were calls within our denomination for the UUA to rid its investment portfolio of all holdings in companies doing business with the military. Subsequent analysis indicated that approximately one-thousandth of our Association's portfolio involved defense business, most of it for fuel. In 1972, the UUA trustees concluded that to totally divest of investments in corporations doing business with the Defense Department might be the wrong approach; holding nominal investments would permit the Association to work from within at stockholders meetings.

The UUA Department of Education and Social Concern took numerous actions pertaining to corporate practices, including the following examples:

- In 1972, we notified the board chairmen of Exxon and Consolidated Edison of concerns regarding their social policies, especially pollution and Exxon's proposed drilling activities off the coast of Angola in southwest Africa.

- In 1973, the UUA participated in Campaign Honeywell, urging that company to cease developing and producing antipersonnel weapons.

- In April 1973, UUA staff member Margaret Williams testified in Washington before the House Foreign Affairs Subcommittee on Africa regarding Exxon's proposed investment in offshore oil operations in Angola. She mentioned during her testimony that the UUA had begun to follow more closely the social policies of such corporations.

- In 1974, the UUA joined a broad coalition that included Protestant and Catholic agencies in challenging the equal opportunity policies of major U.S. corporations. The coalition filed stockholder resolutions concerning equal opportunity for women and racial minorities with nine corporations; the UUA filed a resolution with Ford Motor Company.

Our denomination worked with the Interfaith Center for Corporate Responsibility on social aspects of corporate practices in the spring of 1977. Unitarian Universalists across the continent raised a number of issues at stockholders meetings, including disclosure of nuclear power information, guidelines for marketing infant formula in third world countries, disclosure of foreign military sales, corporate expansion in South Africa, and cessation of bank loans to Chile. All those issues were the subjects of stockholder resolutions that our Association filed.

Other Issues

In September 1972, the UUA sent letters to all our suppliers urging them to cooperate with Project Equality, a national interfaith program that focused on obtaining equal-opportunity commitments from cooperating organizations and businesses about their hiring and employment practices. By early December, we had received signed commitment forms from forty-three providers. For institutional members, the group also conducted evaluations of equal-opportunity practices at specific hotels they might plan to patronize. In June 1974, the UUA trustees voted to expand our denomination's participation in Project Equality by making annual payments for institutional membership and for reviews of hotels used by the UUA.

Earlier the same year, I testified at the Federal Trade Commission hearings on funeral practices, stating that there was a compelling need for consumer protection from unrestricted practices of the funeral industry. I urged adoption of the proposed FTC rule that involved eleven specific aspects of current industry practices, emphasizing that the regulations were "needed to prevent the exploitation and abuse of consumers." I cited specific instances of funeral director abuses reported by Unitarian Universalist ministers and noted that the funeral industry deals with consumers when, because of personal grief and unusual time pressure, they are most vulnerable to unfair sales efforts. The UUA trustees subsequently approved a resolution urging the FTC to implement its proposed regulations and specifically named nine practices that should be prohibited.

Thirty-one religious groups formed the Religious Committee for ERA in 1976 because ratification of the Equal Rights Amendment to the U.S. Constitution by the states had lagged. The amendment provided that "equality of rights under the law shall not be denied or abridged by the United States or any state on account of sex." Both congressional houses passed the ERA in 1972, but ratification by thirty-eight states was required for it to become effective. The UUA and the Unitarian Universalist Women's Federation were affiliates of the committee, which focused on working with church members in five key states. Representatives from the UUA and Women's Federation participated in the committee's national meeting in September 1976.

Also in 1976, the Association became a participating organization in the National Coalition Against Handguns. The director of our Washington Office for Social Concern was a member of its executive committee.

Though many of us at UUA headquarters frequently engaged in public actions relating to national and international issues, I didn't consider those actions to be the most effective means toward fulfilling our denomination's commitment to social responsibility. In the keynote address at our annual United Nations seminar in March 1971 (see the chapter "UUA Offices"), I welcomed the opportunity to make my views more explicit. I noted that during the early months of my presidency I had deliberately refrained from "issuing noble proclamations of what we obviously believe and practice, or vigorous appeals for action in those areas where I know most of our congregations already are committed. . . ." I continued,

> I have become aware in recent months that a few voices have questioned the commitment of the Unitarian Universalist Association to the cause of social justice and world community. While we have been engaged in reorganizing our denominational structures to provide basic services to congregations and still operate on current income and repay an enormous debt, we have been accused of fiddling with the machinery while the world burns. While we have been struggling—successfully, I believe—to provide a sound, basic level of serv-

ices for our congregations within our means, we have been accused of trying to preserve institutions as the sirens scream. While we have been seeking a clearer awareness and articulation of our identity, we are accused of gazing at our navels while the environment crumbles.

I acknowledged that as president of the UUA I had "taken an intentionally different approach regarding UUA endeavors to help alleviate social cancer," and went on to say,

> I have done so because I believe our UUA efforts in social action should relate more directly to the day-by-day activities of our many congregations within their own communities. I believe the most important measure of any denominational program is its influence with respect to local congregations, and the influence of those congregations in turn upon our larger society. Today we have more, not fewer, professional staff people at the UUA actively working in social action than was true two years ago. We are continuing to speak out as a denominational voice on a variety of issues, but we are attempting to focus strongly on the individual congregation as the primary effective unit in social action. If social action is not taking place in and stemming from local communities, then in practical terms we deceive ourselves in believing we have an effective social action program.

In March 1977, UUA moderator Joseph Fisher gave an address at First and Second Church in Boston. In response to questions, he said,

> Our appetites have sometimes outrun our resources. We have tried to remake the world with three or four people and $1,500. . . . Perhaps there's been a little too much jumping on social action bandwagons. There's a shrillness in us that needs to be muted. . . . As religious liberals we must beware undertaking activities that are, subconsciously perhaps, no more than an escape from personal problems into frenetic

social action. . . . I believe there should be an individual, highly personal basis for participation in social action, as well as an outgoing quality. Social action should be "inner directed" as well as "other directed."

In his formal address, Dr. Fisher cautioned,

Let us make certain not to undertake activities in the absence of deep personal motivation, as well as recognition of general social need. Above all let us not be negative only, but let our protest always be accompanied by positive, practical programs—remembering that nothing is as powerful, or as responsible, as a practical program that comes from the joining of deep, personal religious impulse to a worthy social cause. Let us choose our lines of activity carefully and then pursue them vigorously. As always, the problem of free men and women is to exercise their freedom wisely and responsibly [regarding whether and when to do what. That involves] excruciating choices that test a person's religion and common sense. In these choices and how we make them is the essence of social responsibility.

Those words of Joseph Fisher, spoken three months before we ended our terms of office, encapsulate his knowledge and advice about the social-action process—grounded in decades of experience as a leader who strove to remedy social needs, held a number of public offices, participated actively in his congregation, and served as UUA moderator for twelve years. The words also reflect my experiences as a parish minister and community activist in the fifties and sixties as well as UUA president for eight years.

I believe Dr. Fisher was attempting in that address to convey for the future benefit of our denomination, which he loved, the way to effectively implement our impulse toward social responsibility and pitfalls to avoid. Drawing on his own experiences of pain as well as progress, he expressed the essence of how members in a voluntary group achieve effective social action. I hope the spirit and the letter of those words remain with us through the years to come.

Leaving

ON THE AFTERNOON before I left my office at 25 Beacon Street for the final time, I met with the members of our headquarters staff to say good-bye. I expressed my gratitude to them for performing so well day after day, despite limited resources and adverse circumstances. I told them that they were a good staff, and that with people like them there at headquarters I could walk away without looking back, with no feeling of guilt as I departed.

I'm still aware today that those staff members—as well as countless other people in our denomination—were an essential part of whatever I might have accomplished as UUA president. I continue to be grateful to them.

Shortly after that meeting, I gave my last annual report to a General Assembly and shared some thoughts—both positive and negative—about the past eight years. I mentioned my regret for having to cut the UUA budget every year, and particularly for the resulting reorganizations in 1969 and 1975 and the individual traumas that necessarily resulted. I felt good about the Committee on Education for Professional Religious Leadership and the decision, after much study and some agony, to set up a continuing body concerned with the education of our professional religious leaders. I was encouraged that more of our members were interested in extending our numbers and influence as a denomination and that we finally had begun achieving our annual program fund goals.

I expressed my strong appreciation for the efforts of people in our denomination to be "a voice for freedom of speech, press, privacy, religion, and association over these years—and a voice for individual liberty and the functioning of democracy before Watergate." What the people in our denomination did to resist government intrusion on constitutional liberties back in the early seventies is something I'll always remember.

In concluding the brief report, I noted there had been a turning point in our denomination about two years earlier, and since that time we had experienced a dominant tone of optimism and hope and a level of vitality not evident before; there was a constructive climate among lay people and clergy; the morale of our ministers was much higher; people believed problems were solvable; and there was a renewed interest in personal religious growth and depth.

My departing words to the General Assembly were: "My hope for this religious movement is that it will ever be blessed by the faith and dedication of its members, by unswerving loyalty to the highest, and by a common honest striving to touch the eternal in our lives."

In writing this book, three insights have become clear to me. One is that, except for meeting and marrying Nancy, the most powerful force in my life has been Unitarian Universalist religion. The second is that no one can change the past: The only constructive reason to dwell on the past is to learn from it.

The third is that this denomination of ours is an ever-changing religious enterprise. Yet running through the change is the sinew of the principles that cause us to be as a religious movement. Those principles constitute the dynamism, as well as the parameters, of change.

We have come a startlingly long way since our direct institutional ancestors, the Puritans of Massachusetts. I believe we will flourish even beyond where we are today—if we welcome the dynamism, are mindful of the parameters of change, and remain dedicated to the principles that cause us to be.

Acronyms

AUA	American Unitarian Association
BAC	Black Affairs Council
BAWA	Black and White Action
BHF	Black Humanist Fellowship
BIC	Black Affairs Council Investment Corporation
BUUC	Black Unitarian Universalist Caucus
BVCC	Basic Venture Capital Corporation
CLF	Church of the Larger Fellowship
CUC	Canadian Unitarian Council
FORWARD	Freedom of Religion Will Advance Real Democracy
IARF	International Association for Religious Freedom
LREDA	Liberal Religious Education Directors Association
LRY	Liberal Religious Youth

MEC	Ministerial Education Commission
NCC	National Council of Churches
SRL	Student Religious Liberals
UUA	Unitarian Universalist Association
UUMA	Unitarian Universalist Ministers Association
UUSC	Unitarian Universalist Service Committee
UU-UNO	Unitarian Universalist United Nations Office
UUWF	Unitarian Universalist Women's Federation

Acknowledgments

I'm grateful to the following people who gave me special encouragement to undertake this written account: Dwight Brown, William Duffy, James Elson, John Hurley, Peter Houck, Peter Raible, Warren Ross, Carl Scovel, and Tom Stites.

Jerry Gabert, Janet Hayes, John Hurley, Erika Nonken, and Marty Scherstuhl were particularly helpful in assisting me to obtain information. I am also indebted to Frances O'Donnell, curator of manuscripts and archives in the Andover-Harvard theological library of Harvard Divinity School, for her personal attention and helpfulness with part of my research.

I thank the following people for their invaluable assistance with specific portions of the text:

William B. Duffy Jr. for reviewing the chapter "BUUC Court Proceedings," and segments of the chapters "Pentagon Papers" and "Veatch and Holdeen," to confirm their accuracy to the best of his knowledge. As UUA special counsel engaged expressly to work on Pentagon Papers matters, and subsequently UUA associate counsel and then general counsel, Mr. Duffy was closely involved in the legal proceedings described.

Robert E. Senghas for reviewing three of the last four paragraphs in the chapter "Veatch and Holdeen" to confirm their accuracy. Rev. Senghas was UUA executive vice president from 1974 to 1979 and has served for many years as a member of the body that designates beneficiaries of the annual income from two Holdeen trusts.

Rev. Diether Gehrmann and Dorle Gehrmann for providing some of the information about the IARF in the chapter "International Activities" and reviewing it for accuracy.

Rev. Carl Scovel for sharing documents associated with his work as chairperson of the Ministerial Education Commission, as well as reviewing the related portions of the "Professional Religious Leadership" Chapter for accuracy.

David Pohl for providing most of the data included in six of the final nine paragraphs of the chapter "Professional Religious Leadership" and for reviewing them to ensure their accuracy. Rev. Pohl was appointed UUA ministerial settlement director in 1971 and subsequently served as director of the Department of Ministry until 1993.

The Reverends Max Gaebler and Earl Holt for providing some of the information about BAWA in the chapter "Associate Organizations," and Rev. Gaebler for reviewing that section to confirm its accuracy.

Others who have demonstrated their support during the course of writing this book include Pat and J. T. Hundley, Mary Krebbs, Joyce Lehmann, Helen and Eugene Pickett, Catherine and Josh Pinto, Lynda and Francisco Pinto-Torres, Martha Pohl, Jean and Sterling Weaver, Amy and Tom West, Charles West, and Robert West Jr.

I'm indebted especially to Mary Benard for her talented editing assistance, and to Patricia Frevert, the director of Skinner

House Books. But honesty compels me to testify that my deepest gratitude is reserved for the person who not only supported me with prodigious amounts of love and care and forbearance during the three years of my writing this book and eight years that constitute its subject, but throughout all fifty-six years of our marriage, Nancy West.

Index